Books by David Halberstam

The Noblest Roman

The Making of a Quagmire

One Very Hot Day

The Unfinished Odyssey of Robert Kennedy

The Unfinished Odyssey
of Robert Kennedy

The Unfinished Odyssey of Robert Kennedy

David Halberstam

 Random House

New York

Acknowledgments

Many people assisted in the writing of this book; a list of everyone who cooperated would be hopelessly long. From Senator Kennedy's staff I am particularly indebted to Frank Mankiewicz and Fred Dutton; among colleagues, Dick Harwood, Jimmy Breslin, and Pete Hamill for their coverage of incidents where I was not present. At *Harper's Magazine* Willie Morris and Bob Kotlowitz provided aid and encouragement; Lucille Beachy of *Newsweek* was generous in providing material on the campaign. In addition, William Shannon's *The Heir Apparent* and Dick Schaap's *R.F.K.* were particularly helpful.

This book is for

Bill Barry

and Dick Tuck

Odyssey: ... 2. ... A long series
of wanderings, esp when
filled with notable experiences,
hardships, etc.

*The Random House Dictionary of the
English Language,* Unabridged Edition

The Unfinished Odyssey
of Robert Kennedy

I

In the late summer of 1967, a time of growing social turbulence and dissatisfaction in America, a young liberal named Allard Lowenstein went to visit his senator from New York, Robert Kennedy. A few years before, no two men in the Democratic party could have been more dissimilar: Lowenstein was a reformer, indeed an almost promiscuous reformer. A protégé of Eleanor Roosevelt and quick to enter her name in every conversation, he was identified with a vast list, perhaps too vast a list, of good and decent causes. Indeed it was not a liberal cause unless it were championed by Al Lowenstein. He was exactly the kind of person that Robert Kennedy, just a few years before, had most despised. Then Robert Kennedy had been the tough guy, ramrodding through his brother's nomination and election, and the reformers, God, at the beginning the reformers were almost worse than the Republicans. They hemmed and hawed; they talked too much and said too little; and they loved Stevenson. The reformers were too soft; too issue-prone; too—and this was the worst word yet—predictable. In 1960 Kennedy had exploded before New York's finest and purest reformers, saying, "Gentlemen, I don't give a damn if the state and county organizations survive after November and I don't give a damn if you survive. I want to elect John F. Kennedy President." And they loved that, though in later years when they thought warm thoughts about the Kennedy Presidency they would not remember Robert Kennedy's hard work and vital contribution to that end, but rather the harshness of his words.

Kennedy would have considered Lowenstein one of the worst of them. He was very closely associated with the old New Dealers, always running around Mississippi with black people, and had gone to South Africa and written a book about it. Indeed his liberalism was so pure and so all-encompassing that his friends gently and affectionately mocked it. According to Lowenstein legend, a friend once called his house and asked for him—"Al just left for Spain," replied his mother. "You know he never did like that General Franco. . . ."

By 1967, however, the intensity of social upheaval had brought Lowenstein and Kennedy closer together. Lowenstein was devoting himself to heightening and sharpening the protest against Lyndon Johnson. Ambitious and deeply committed, a rare moralist-activist, and a member of the board of the ADA (though more radical and less anti-Communist than men ten years older than he), he would appear on campus after campus, a veteran student leader, perhaps the oldest in America, giving a focal point to the growing discontent. Whenever *The New York Times* ran a full-page ad saying "Rhodes Scholars Oppose War in Vietnam," or "Mister President, Peace Corps Returnees Oppose Your War," or "College Editors Oppose," etc., it was sure to be the work of Al Lowenstein. He had become truly evangelical on the campus, taking the dissenting and the alienated, telling them, really beseeching them, that yes, they could still work within the system, it could still be done, that protest against the war could be effectively registered within the system. Anyone who saw him during those days would remember the almost feverish quality to his work and remember asking him if it were hard to get kids interested in his crusade, and his answering that the only problem was bringing them back into the system; that no one knew how deeply alienated they were. Then he would excuse himself and fly off to Berkeley for two days and from there to Oregon and from there to Idaho. Al Lowenstein had gone everywhere in 1967, haunting Lyndon Johnson, and he had been properly smeared by Government officials. Peace Corps public-information officers had gone as far as to leak material insinuating that he was very left wing. Now, in the late summer, Lowenstein was trying to convince Robert Kennedy to run for President against Lyndon Johnson.

Kennedy, once a conservative, then an unannounced and reluctant liberal whose credentials were regularly challenged by more orthodox liberals, was by 1967 pursuing a course of increasing radicalism—proffering more radical ideas and taking on, from people like Lowenstein, more radical advice. His course was not so much a consistent philosophy as it was the application of his puritanism (what one friend called his perpetual sense of outrage) to a changing America. The more he looked, the more his vision of the country changed; darkening as he saw more of the inequities and more of the failures. The country was in transition politically, and curiously, so was he.

By both intent and heredity Kennedy had become the leader of the honorable opposition in the Democratic party; the leading critic of the administration's treatment of the ghettos, the leading critic of a great Pandora's box of social problems, and if not the leading critic of the war, the most important politically. When J. William Fulbright attacked the war it annoyed the President, but when Robert Kennedy attacked the war it meant that armies might march. The young liberals and radicals in their thirties and forties, and the college students, those who were staying within the system, no longer turned to Hubert Humphrey for their leadership, but to Robert Kennedy.

Lowenstein, this day, was telling Kennedy that the

time had come when the speeches on Vietnam in the Senate,
and the articles for *Look* magazine on the ghetto were no
longer enough. It was 1967-going-on-1968 and the army,
the vast network of conspirators, was ready to march. It
had decided that despite the foremost myth of American
politics—Rule One: You cannot unseat a sitting president
of your own party—Johnson must and, more important,
could be beaten. Lowenstein felt that the issues were far
too great to let traditional party loyalty and regulations
dominate. Times were different now. The network was in
action and was very strong within the Democratic party;
Johnson's invincibility was a myth, he could be beaten. The
polls showed otherwise, but the polls reflected the mythology. The politicians said otherwise, but as John Kenneth
Galbraith, the head of Americans for Democratic Action and
another pioneer in the Bust Johnson movement, had said
with great insight and accuracy early in 1967, "This is a
year when the people are right and the politicians are
wrong." It would be a new and different coalition, Lowenstein told Kennedy; it would have to be done outside the
party machinery. It would make powerful enemies for
Kennedy, but they would be older men; men who, given
the changing nature of American politics, would be less
influential politically year by year; whereas the friends he
would make would be young people and increasingly influential. But it could be done. Johnson was a hollow man
politically; no one, and this was crucial, was for him or
liked him. The war in the year ahead would get worse,
turning more and more hawks to doves, making the opposition more and more respectable. Indeed doing the right
thing would be politically advantageous. But the important
thing, Lowenstein emphasized, was the nature of the issues
—the war and the ghettos. They were issues of moral imperative, so serious that they did not permit waiting until
1972.

They were good friends now, and had been since 1966 when Kennedy, planning to take a trip to South Africa, had prepared a speech with which he was not totally satisfied. Someone recommended Lowenstein as a South African expert and he, as was the Kennedy wont, was summoned imperiously. He could not come, he said, because he was taking Norman Thomas, who was almost blind, to the Dominican Republic. For God's sake, Norman Thomas!, Kennedy said, exasperated—for to him Norman Thomas was *then* and this was *now*—get someone else to take Norman Thomas to the Dominican Republic. It was only at Kennedy Airport that Lowenstein did find someone to escort the old man; and he left to join Kennedy. He looked at the South Africa speech and did not hesitate to tell the Senator that he found it appalling, representing basically the view of the South African Bureau of Tourism—a totally white viewpoint —the conclusion of which was that the South Africans must do a little better by their Kaffirs. Lowenstein criticized the speech sharply and bluntly, and got on the phone to call some South African students attending colleges in the East. When they were assembled, they too rallied, testifying to the fact that it was a disastrous speech; it was accordingly changed, though much to the regret of the South African government. Disliking sycophants, Kennedy was delighted with Lowenstein and his display. They became friends. Kennedy came to value Lowenstein as an extra-intelligence operative, admiring his commitment and idealism, and appreciating the fact that Lowenstein was well connected among some radicals and students. He could help Kennedy interpret the relative merits of the tribes in that particular jungle; a jungle in which he was particularly interested.

But Allard Lowenstein was not the first to tell him to run for the Presidency. Half the people Kennedy met were telling him to run, and the other half, of course, were telling him not to. The dilemma had been with him for some time.

At an ADA meeting in 1967, he had sat with a group of distinguished liberals, all frustrated by the war and their party's control of the presidency. One of the men had said that the great strategy for 1968 would be to have a peace plank in the platform; yes, Lyndon Johnson running on a peace plank. Kennedy had turned and said, "When was the last time you heard of rallying millions of people to a plank?" Robert Lowell, the poet, had bitterly challenged him earlier in the year, saying that Kennedy's ambivalent behavior was disgraceful, and asking what it really was that Kennedy was running for, the presidency of Harvard? Kennedy agreed thoroughly, noting that the way things were going he would be very lucky to get even that.

Kennedy in fact had thought about the race a great deal and had talked to many people; friends from the Kennedy administration, the bosses who had helped put John Kennedy in office. Though he was getting active and enthusiastic encouragement from friends whom he associated with social issues and whose judgment he trusted on these issues, he was getting just the opposite from people whose judgment he trusted on political matters—the people he had always turned to in the past, the professionals. They told him that first: no, it couldn't be done, and second: he would destroy himself in the party if he tried—he would never be forgiven by the party faithful, and would be charged with dividing the party (which was of course already hopelessly divided: the party regulars vs. virtually everyone else). Though this was to be a year in which social issues and new social forces would finally surface politically, Robert Kennedy had not yet realized that; and he sided with the political judgment of the pros. He admired the moral judgment, the sincerity, of people like Lowenstein, but he had talked with Mayor Daley, and Governor Y, and Chairman Z, and they had all said the same thing: you can't do it, it's not the year, you must wait. We like you; we loved your brother; and we think favorably of you for 1972, but you can't do it. And so Robert Kennedy passed this on to Lowenstein: I'm sorry, he said, I can't do it. And Lowenstein, an intense and consummately serious young man, looked at him for a long time and then answered: "The people who think that the future and the honor of this country are at stake because of Vietnam don't give a shit what Mayor Daley and Governor Y and Chairman Z think. We're going to do it, and we're going to win, and it's a shame you're not with us, because you could have been President." Then they shook hands rather sadly and parted.

That was how the 1968 campaign began for Robert Kennedy: it began badly. Later he realized this as his natural constituency slipped away. In late March, after he had finally entered the race, he was on a bus with Lowenstein in upstate New York. Overhearing someone say that Lowenstein had left Eugene McCarthy and had come over to him, Kennedy excitedly grabbed Lowenstein, anticipating that this move might bring some of the kids around to his side, but only to find that he had heard incorrectly. Impressed with Lowenstein's loyalty to McCarthy, and feeling somewhat sad for himself, later during that ride he took up a pad and scribbled a note to his friend:

> For Al, who knew the lessons of Emerson and taught it to the rest of us: "They did not yet see and thousands of young men as hopeful, now crowding to the barriers of their careers, do not yet see that if a single man plant himself on his convictions and then abide, the huge world will come round to him." From his friend Bob Kennedy.

The coalition which was forming in the country in mid-1967 was a loose one, people like Lowenstein and Galbraith, some of the key officials of the California Democratic Councils, a few eggheads here and there, and occasionally a dissenting party official. The coalition was strong on the campuses, for it was there that the issue of Vietnam had first bloomed politically. It had started with the teach-ins in 1965. The issue had been taken up by white middle-class kids and intensified by the fact that it was not just an intangible moral issue, but indeed a very tangible one—the draft having given it great immediacy. In 1967 the issue had not yet touched some of the traditional centers of the Democratic party such as the labor unions or the party apparatus itself. Though there were places where party officials sensed its presence, they remained silent, for fear that discussion would heighten the issue and the Republicans would end up exploiting it. The party professionals by and large would not accept the fact that it was already an expanding issue. They would sample the temperature of the water as they always had, largely by talking to people very much like themselves, and they would find little if any dissent among what they considered real people. The average non-intellectual American at that time may have felt doubts about the war, but he was being extremely cautious about expressing them. He might have suspected that the war was one great, terrible, stupid disaster, but when asked would perhaps mumble something about protecting Thailand. The professionals, in 1967, did not talk to students, nor to the middle class in the suburbs; they saw little of what was happening.

But the coalition was convinced that this was not a lost cause. The country was ripe for an unorthodox political movement. They believed Johnson to be a war president who could only drag the country deeper into the war and they vowed that their party would not be his vehicle if they could help it. These men were driven by their own moral imperative. They saw the war as a quagmire, the country hopelessly bogged down in a useless, hopeless conflict which could not be won, and they felt that the longer the war went on, the more dangerous and more isolated Johnson became. Writing now, in 1968, it is hard to re-create the atmosphere. They saw a steady migration of doubters from Washington's official circles, and when McNamara left in 1967, they were terrified. Though McNamara had earlier been the symbol of the war, McNamara's War, they thought that he had, by the end, become a voice of sanity. It was rumored in dark corners that McNamara was a dove in hawk's clothing, and the departure of the Good McNamara proved to them the insanity of the administration. They also witnessed the steady ascension of the sycophants, the people who told the President what he wanted to hear. It was no longer a credibility gap, but rather a reality gap, which existed in Washington. The President had never been known as a man to honor those who brought him bad news, and that most human weakness of his—under the pressure of the war's becoming a dangerous one—was becoming worse daily. At a small dinner party for Everett Martin, a distinguished *Newsweek* correspondent just back from two years in Vietnam, Walt Whitman Rostow, the man who chose what the President would see on Vietnam and chose it very carefully indeed, managed to spend a full evening without ever once acknowledging that Martin had been to Vietnam—no small feat. The dissenters in late 1967 were not normal political opponents, they were men genuinely terrified about the course of American action. They were frightened by Johnson's personal identification with the war—he chose every bombing site, he flew every mission—and were uneasy not only with where their country was, but where it was going.

They were also convinced that the alleged hawkish orientation of the country was misleading; that a lot of hawks were only skin deep; and once dovishness was given any kind of serious political outlet, there would be an exodus from hawk to dove. "Our advantage," said Galbraith, "was that even if there were more hawks than doves, the hawks didn't really believe what they said. It was easy to turn them around."

The coalition had sought Kennedy first for he was the ideal candidate. He was not only the logical leader on many of the vital issues, but he was by far the candidate with the broadest base of power. He had the Kennedy name, the Kennedy glamour, and he would be able to hold some of the blue-collar people who might otherwise be outside their coalition because of anti-Negro or pro-war feeling. (Significantly, Lyndon Johnson received his biggest ovations in 1967 at labor-union meetings whereas it was almost impossible for him to visit any campus.) The choice of Kennedy was not an instance of Camelotism or Kennedyism. The Camelot people, the people who had had it very good in the early sixties and who wanted a restoration, were as yet uneasy about the race. They wanted the restoration, but they didn't want to blow it. They were willing to wait until 1972 and thought the country should also be willing. Most of the people pulling for Kennedy to make the race were doing so not because it was Camelot, but precisely because it was not—because Robert Kennedy, in the past few years, had very deliberately taken over the leadership of the disenfranchised and the dissatisfied in America. These people were tough minded. They traveled throughout the country and saw glimmers of political responsiveness that others, sitting in Washington talking to themselves, did not see. For if in those days the average political reporter scorned and underestimated what Lowenstein and Galbraith and others were doing, it was also true that they did not travel as much as these men; and when they did, they talked more often with other political reporters and professional politicians rather than with the people on the campuses and in the middle-class suburbs.

Failing with Kennedy, the coalition started looking around for another candidate. There was the possibility of General James Gavin, the ex-paratrooper who had been making dovish noises, but when they spoke with him, Gavin said he was a Republican. There were some well-known doves in the Senate such as Frank Church and George Mc-Govern and Wayne Morse, but all three had tough fights for reelection on their hands. McGovern, one of the most decent men in the Senate, suggested Lowenstein go out to South Dakota to sample the waters and decide whether he could run for both the Senate and the presidency. Lowenstein did, and reluctantly concluded that McGovern would have to run two different races with two different tones, something that might prove at best embarrassing, and at worst, disastrous. McGovern did say, however, that if no one else would do it they should come back and see him. Then they turned to Eugene McCarthy of Minnesota, perhaps not as outspoken as some of the others on the war, but nonetheless a member of the liberal Senate group, and a man, and this was crucial, who was not up for re-election. McCarthy, when approached by the Turks, was neither messianic nor coy. Yes; he thought someone should make the race, but no; he did not think he was the best choice. He suggested Robert Kennedy as a likelier candidate, a man with a broader base, but he did say that if no one else would run, he would make the race. "There comes a time when an honorable man simply has to raise the flag," he said.

McCarthy seemed an unlikely man to challenge the most active, restless President in recent history. He was a particularly calm, low-keyed man, and even his friends sometimes suspected he had something of an energy gap. He was a liberal (with a few bad marks from the ADA for some of his oil-depletion votes—"Gene is a little soft on minor issues," explained one friend), an ex-professor, and a devout, almost mystic, Catholic. Later in the campaign his aides sometimes complained to each other that he was not available; he could not be reached either physically or spiritually; he was in one of his mystic moods. He was witty; sharp and acid in his comments. Describing the government in South Vietnam, he said it was "not a dictatorship, but a public-relations job." When asked by a reporter what he would do if elected, he mimicked the Eisenhower vow of 1960, saying, "I will go to the Pentagon." He obviously looked down upon most of the men he dealt with in politics, including his colleagues in the Senate, and regarded much of the press with considerable distaste. He was also obviously bright: he would listen to someone for a minute or two and then turn off, having absorbed as much as he thought he wanted to and having become bored. Yet it was part of his particular appeal that his admirers and his critics were equally divided as to whether he was the humblest man ever to enter American politics, or the most arrogant. Indeed it was a distinction that McCarthy himself was well aware of: "There is a fine line," he said once, "between humility and the ultimate arrogance." He could be caustic and witty, and at times his humor bordered on bitterness and one sensed in him a certain petulance; as if the American system had never really given him his due. He was at once the kind of man who could inspire the youth of America with his New Hampshire campaign, bringing them to a feverish pitch of activity, and then note afterward that this primary had proved that all one needed in American politics was a candidate and someone to drive him—a statement which did not endear him to these thousands of young volunteers.

McCarthy had had national ambitions before and, for a variety of reasons, he was not unreceptive when, in late 1967, he was asked to run. In 1960 he had told friends, in one of those half jokes which are much more serious than anyone really intends, that he was a better candidate than Hubert Humphrey, Jack Kennedy, or Stuart Symington, "because [he was] twice as liberal as Hubert, twice as Catholic as Jack and twice as smart as Stu." He never favored the Kennedy candidacy before the nomination, looking down upon Kennedy, as many of the Stevenson disciples did at that time, as something of an intellectual lightweight. In addition, McCarthy, a serious lay intellectual and a not entirely secular man, tended to look down on Kennedy's religious feeling which he thought was less serious than his own. This angered the Kennedys, and Robert Kennedy in particular. The bad feeling was sharpened by McCarthy's behavior at the Los Angeles convention. He arrived there as a supporter of Lyndon Johnson and yet, when the Stevenson boom started, it was he who made the nominating speech. It was probably the best of his career: "Do not turn your back on this man who made us proud to be Democrats." The moment was regarded by most liberals as the high point of the convention—a moment of the heart and brain working together—but was regarded by the Kennedy camp as part of a cynical Johnsonian cabal; a move to halt Jack Kennedy and nominate Lyndon Johnson. Indeed it was a deliberate part of Johnson's strategy to use Stevenson to stop Kennedy on the first ballot. Recalling this incident, in 1967, McCarthy remembered that he preferred Johnson to Kennedy but recalled some of his doubts. "I told people I was for Johnson for prime minister which is a pretty good indication of my reservations. I was sure he could get as much out of a given situation as any man could, but I had doubts about whether he could project the country into a certain direction. That's why I said prime minister—

the prime minister operates within the pattern of his party, subject to his cabinet and the path the party sets, and thus tries to get the most out of that path. It's not as personalized as the presidency. I was wrong about Kennedy though; he did have an institutionalized sense of the presidency, whereas with Johnson you have this terribly personalized presidency—'they're all my helicopters.' (A reference to an incident during which a young airman said 'this is your helicopter, sir,' as the President was about to board the wrong one. The President explained to the airman the error of his ways; 'they're all my helicopters, son.')"

McCarthy and Johnson had stayed reasonably good friends during the Kennedy administration (neither was an insider in those days), and in 1964, when Johnson was dangling the vice-presidency all over Washington, McCarthy was one of those interested. Indeed Senate aficionados attribute one of McCarthy's soft oil votes to vice-presidential hopes. McCarthy was convenient for Johnson in those days too; the President could keep Robert Kennedy off the ticket and still end up with a liberal Catholic. McCarthy rose to the bait. Johnson delighted in playing Humphrey and McCarthy against each other; there was one particularly banal television show in which they outdid each other flattering the President. There was a certain quality of low-level humiliation to it and finally McCarthy, realizing what was happening, sent a telegram to the President, withdrawing. Thus he spared himself, as Senator Thomas Dodd did not, being a puppet in the very last minute of the marionette show. (William S. White, Johnson's favorite columnist, later wrote that McCarthy was still bitter over the incident and that this had made him more willing to run in 1968. "What meat then is feeding this improbable Caesar, Eugene McCarthy?" intoned White, no small authority on Caesars himself, ". . . a fierce fire of ambition, fanned by the hot, fanatic thirst that now grips the throats of the American peacenik movement.)"

But now in 1968, after McCarthy entered, the feeling between Kennedy and McCarthy—the two key men who would be in opposition to Johnson—was still surprisingly hostile. This became a vital factor as the campaign developed and minor points became major ones, and the uneasiness and mutual suspicion developed into genuine hard feeling. At the start, when McCarthy first went in, they wished each other well and spoke well of one another. Though Kennedy still talked ambivalently about supporting Johnson, he gave McCarthy good advice about New Hampshire; enter and run against the machine. And McCarthy spoke well of Kennedy, regularly denying that he was his stalking horse. However McCarthy did concede, as he told this reporter in early December, that, because the issue involved was so great, if Kennedy finally did enter, he would probably move aside. There would be no problem there; Kennedy had a larger base. But underneath there was considerable hostility. McCarthy regarded Kennedy as an intellectual inferior, an arrogant and pushy young man cashing in on his brother's myth and his family's money. One always sensed that a good deal of McCarthy's hostility toward the American political system, and this hostility existed, came from the advantages he felt it gave the rich. He felt his own natural resources were greater than Kennedy's, and if wealth were not a factor, there would be no comparison.

Robert Kennedy, for his part, retained a blind spot as far as John Kennedy was concerned. Those who had helped him (such as Hubert Humphrey; there was a curious sense of sympathy and friendship for Humphrey because after the Kennedy's had fought him, and had broken him in West Virginia, Humphrey had rallied to campaign for Jack Kennedy and had wept at the news of his death) had a special place, and those who had downgraded him were rarely reprieved; and McCarthy had downgraded him. But it went deeper; Kennedy, the evangelist, thought McCarthy a cynical man, a lazy man; and the part of Kennedy which loved power was uneasy about McCarthy's course. Sometimes he saw in it elements of another Henry Wallace campaign (a curious aspect of Kennedy, for he himself sought the very people that McCarthy had), and he wondered whether McCarthy was stronger than some of the people swirling around him. In late December their relationship was still cordial but suspicious; Kennedy was still playing Hamlet on whether or not to run. The Kennedy people suggested to McCarthy that he enter New Hampshire and run there and stay out of Massachusetts, which might prove more difficult and which, of course, was regarded as their very own preserve. McCarthy, hearing that, immediately entered Massachusetts. He had not intended to enter New Hampshire until his arm was virtually twisted into it by his own people. There was no mutual ease, and it was to get worse between them. One remembered Kennedy, several months later, preparing to go on *Face the Nation* and going through a mock press conference with aides. Someone, posing as a reporter, asked him, "Senator Kennedy, would you support President Johnson if he is the nominee?" "That's easy," Kennedy said smiling, "but don't ask me whether I would support McCarthy." Fortunately for him no one asked.

The race seemed on the surface a dubious honor in the first place. In late December and early January, Lyndon Johnson appeared to be supreme. He dominated his own party and though his own party was restless, it appeared paralyzed and bound to him by loyalty and tradition. The Republicans might run against him, but it was hard to imagine a Republican candidate running to the left of him on the war and on the ghettos. Johnson appeared to be a war president who would somehow hold the center. Anyone to the left of him would be a super-dove, anyone to the right of him would be a super-hawk. He would try and hold the Negroes with one hand (behind his back), while he would softly work the crime-in-the-streets issue with the other hand. Though the war was not going well, it did not appear to be going badly either, and again, the dissent was within his own party and thus not serious dissent. But Lyndon Johnson was tied to the war, and it was becoming a bitterly unpopular war. Both the nature of the war and the nature of Lyndon Johnson would combine in 1968 to destroy him, and destroy him where he was supposed to be unbeatable, within his own party.

The war. Nothing dominated American life in 1967 and 1968 like the war. It flashed across the television sets each night; it sapped the financial resources of the country and more, it sapped its moral fiber. In a country consumed by serious social problems everything eventually led back to the war; nothing could be done until the war was over. Much of the tension between black and white was directly traceable to the war and the breakdown of poverty programs it had effected; much of the intensifying division between young and old stemmed from youth's opposition to the war. At a time of growing disillusion with American life, a younger generation found many of the inequities of this country difficult to accept. The war somehow seemed to them to symbolize the thrust of American life; and it was Lyndon Johnson's war.

Curiously enough it had been a minor issue in the election of 1964. Vietnam was simply a distant country which Barry Goldwater wanted to defoliate and which Lyndon Johnson thought unworthy of the lives of American boys, particularly because Asian boys should be doing the job. So it was a muffled issue, overshadowed by the overall issue of Goldwaterism: Was Goldwater safe? Wouldn't he just lob one into the Kremlin men's room? Did you want Goldwater's finger on the button? Johnson would ask, and then he'd gnash his own thumb on an imaginary button, and one knew with great relief that Johnson would not do anything foolish, would not push buttons, would not send the Marines anywhere, would not lob grenades into anyone's men's rooms. (The post-election Republican joke was: "They warned me if I voted for Goldwater we would get in a big war, and the Marines would be sent out, and we would bomb North Vietnam; and I voted for Goldwater and they were right.")

But the atmosphere was curiously relaxed in 1964. A reporter just back from Vietnam and covering the political campaign found a surprising lack of interest among the candidates and their staffs about the war, though fateful decisions were near at hand. Everyone seemed to assume that it was going badly or at least not very well, but that somehow it would go away. The campaign went its way; Vietnam was not the issue, Goldwater was. Goldwater destroyed himself as a candidate. Johnson was elected by a landslide on a mandate of peace. The words hawk and dove did not exist together in the modern political lexicon. The thrust of the right wing seemed terminated; they had finally run their very own candidate, with disastrous results for the Republican party. Now the country seemed curiously united; ready, after many years of delay, to turn this great restless powerhouse of a President loose on long neglected urban and racial problems. Johnson, though not beloved by the liberal columnists, was respected by them. They described him as a healing man and America, God knew, had enough things to heal. Yet the day after his landslide victory aides placed on his desk a list of targets to be bombed in the north—thus assuring, at its very beginning, the end of the Great Society, the destruction of Johnson's presidential years, and his downfall in 1968. For though the issue had been avoided during the campaign, the problems had not gone away; they were all there. All the agonizing decisions of Indochina, delayed ten years, finally had to be confronted —whether the president be Lyndon Johnson, Barry Goldwater or John Kennedy. The proxy war, itself a desperate measure, had been going badly for more than a year and a half. Our proxies could barely hold out (indeed that they had held out that long was itself astounding). The Vietcong had reached the point where they were ambushing not just platoons at night, but now battalions, and even regiments, and often in the daytime. Despite all the calm and placid assurances of Secretary McNamara and General Maxwell Taylor, it was obviously only a short time before the whole proxy effort would collapse.

The war in Vietnam is different from other wars, it is not a war for control of terrain. The side with the greater armament, with all the airplanes, could appear for a long time to be stronger than it really was, its kill statistics would be greater, and its political liabilities barely visible (except in the cold sullen eye of a peasant) and for these reasons it had been possible to sweep the problems of Vietnam under the rug. It had made it possible for men in high places to fool themselves and fool men in even higher places, and for the reality to be delayed, again and again, until finally, one day, the problems surface. When they surface to the insider, they do so only after he has already been caught out on a limb—made too many rash statements, too many easy promises and predictions—and gotten himself in a position where he and his vanity are terribly trapped. When they surface to the general public, it is with a deadly finality.

The American commitment to Vietnam began in 1954

after the French had lost their war and the country was
divided. It was the time of Dulles' containment, and the
idea was to create an anti-Communist, anti-colonialist state
in the South. But from the start the idea was doomed; the
Communists had taken over the nationalism of Indochina
during their eight-year war, and now all the dynamism, all
the talent and drive, all the best young men were on their
side, and it would be only a matter of time before that
showed militarily and politically in the South. Frustrated by
the U.S.-Diem decision against holding free elections (Eisenhower had noted very simply at the time that had the elections been held, Ho Chi Minh would have won in the South),
Hanoi, in 1959, began to use its proxies in the South in the
second Indochina war. The American proxy was the Diem
regime, suspicious, increasingly isolated from all other
elements in the country, its base narrowing all the time.
Diem's situation did not improve with the American aid. In
1962 Bernard Fall interviewed Pham Van Dong, the North
Vietnamese prime minister, and asked about Diem's personal position. "It is quite difficult," Dong said. "He is unpopular and the more unpopular he becomes, the more
American aid he will need to remain in power. And the more
American aid he gets, the more of an American puppet he'll
look and the less likely he is to regain popularity."

"That sounds pretty much like a vicious circle," commented Fall.

"No," said Pham Van Dong, "it's a downward spiral."

The Kennedy administration had come into office in
1961. It immediately suffered a series of foreign policy
setbacks—a particularly difficult position for a young president with a razor-thin margin of victory. There was the
Bay of Pigs, Laos, the Berlin Wall, Khrushchev's bullying at
Vienna, and now it looked like Vietnam was about to go
down the drain. Its government clearly could not hold out

much longer despite its own predictions. In addition to their setbacks there was one other quite separate force which drove the Kennedy administration into Vietnam, and this was a basic contempt for the Eisenhower administration. The Kennedy people looked upon their predecessor as flabby, unaware of a changing world, and far too dependent upon military response. It had been ignorant of the subtleties and possibilities of guerrilla warfare in the third world. The Communists, they felt, had been using this effectively against us, and now it would be used against them. They believed that the failure of the Eisenhower administration in Vietnam lay in the fact that the South Vietnamese army had been trained for a conventional war, while it was fighting in reality an unconventional one. There was a certain arrogance to this, a feeling that they were tougher, brighter and more contemporary than the Eisenhower people, and Robert Kennedy was one of the worst offenders. He became the New Frontier's leading student on guerrilla warfare and Green Beretism, the latter being something of a Washington fad.

Kennedy increased the American commitment to Vietnam—there were now 15,000 advisers as opposed to 600 and Americans were now flying dangerous combat missions in helicopters and old World War II fighter bombers. The flag was planted just that much more (Eisenhower, despite all the Dulles bombast, or perhaps precisely because of it, had never bothered to plant the flag; coming back from World War II he had never felt the political pressure to be a hero or to prove his anti-communism that his two successors might feel). The Kennedy escalation was an action taken out of weakness more than anything else. We had escalated to keep from being driven out of Indochina, and at a price— we had involved ourselves that much deeper; it was no longer a highly avoidable war. We had gone in on the recommendation of Maxwell Taylor, Kennedy's special envoy in Vietnam. Galbraith, Kennedy's all-purpose critic, had read the Taylor report at the time, in 1961, and had told the President that it was "a most curious document. It calls for certain changes and aids to the government but notes that given the nature of the government these changes cannot be achieved." Robert Kennedy was always to have ambivalent opinions about the origins of the war in which he was involved, and particularly the role of Taylor who had become a close family friend. In 1964, while covering his campaign for the Senate, I remember Maxwell Taylor's name having come up in conversation. Ethel Kennedy asked, with her usual enthusiasm, "Don't you just love Max Taylor?" I said rather bitterly that I did not, that I thought him one of the most overrated men in American life and that I thought he was one of the men most responsible for a growing tragedy. Ethel turned white, hurt and offended, and moved away. Ed Guthman, the normally good-natured press secretary, grabbed me angrily and said "Goddamit, don't you know better than to criticize Max Taylor to her. What the hell's wrong with you?" We argued sharply and it was a chilly evening the rest of the way. Even in 1968, when Robert Kennedy was one of the major critics of the war, some of the ambivalence remained. When asked about Taylor, he would say with a certain sadness, "Well he was very helpful to President Kennedy. . . . "

There is a particular quality about this war, a quality which was to have a very considerable political effect, albeit a delayed one. For this is a war in which you can fake it. It is not like desert warfare where if one side is stronger than the other, it is painfully apparent the very next day; nor even like conventional war where the evidence is slower to come, but comes nevertheless—an army inching ahead, holding terrain, a mile or two a day. But in guerrilla warfare, military-political warfare, the stronger side, in military-*political* terms, does not hold terrain, it lacks airpower and heavy artillery and thus does not produce statistics which can match those of the weaker side. Indeed most of what it does best is invisible to the Western eye, and particularly to the Western military eye, which is accustomed and trained to look for something entirely different—in this case, something highly misleading. Thus the weaker side can and did, in Vietnam, delude itself into believing that its charts and predictions were true, and that it was winning. Powerful men with powerful vanities were sucked deeper into avoidable mistakes.

This happened in 1962 and 1963 in Vietnam. Slowly in this proxy war our proxies began to lose and lose badly at an ever intensifying rate; the Vietcong becoming more audacious by the day. Thus the booster-shot commitment had, in late 1963 and 1964, come to an end. Very soon a president would have to make the most basic decision of all; a decision which had been postponed through four administrations—all the way in, or all the way out. But this was a subsurface dilemma, it was still not evident to the American public. Nor was it evident to the American politicians— whether by August of 1964 the White House realized it or wanted to realize it is a matter for conjecture; people at a certain point believe what they want to believe. There was a handful of reporters in Vietnam in 1964 and, though the best of them were pessimistic, they hardly represented a major political voice. On the theory that any news was bad news, the administration had long ago decided to tell the public as little as possible about Vietnam. Any candid admission about where the U.S. stood would point to the fact that all previous predictions had been highly fallacious

and would be highly embarrassing to the men already
in power. An administration can talk candidly about the
errors of American foreign policy only if those errors were
made by a previous administration. So, in 1964, the administration kept the reality of the war hidden. What should
have been the dominant issue of the 1964 campaign was
shelved. Johnson was the peace candidate, peace being but
a general thing, and Goldwater was the war candidate. Had
he known of the onrushing dilemma in Vietnam, Goldwater
might have campaigned vigorously for escalation and Johnson might have moved to the left. Had it been as such, he
would have entered the presidency with Vietnam an issue,
with himself a partial dove, and would have still been
elected by a landslide. He had no such luck.

Thus Johnson was elected by a landslide, but on the
key issue of the time he had gotten a free ride, and now he
was afraid of his own mandate. He had postponed the decision, and he had postponed it at the price of his own credibility. From the very moment he escalated, his credibility
was to be put seriously in doubt, particularly within his own
party. He was to start his first full term by creating an issue
which would eventually cost him his second term. He had
not trusted the American people, and this set a pattern
which was to haunt him. Now, newly elected, he had to
deal with the immensity of the problem. He was elected
a peace candidate and yet he had a special vision of himself;
he saw himself somehow as a figure in *High Noon*. "Sell
the Johnson image as one of a big tall tough Texan," he told
Pierre Salinger in 1960. In truth he was not a particularly
good rider, and his World War II Silver Star was a bogus
one. As for the war, he did not see it in terms of the modern
world, as a struggle in an underdeveloped country in which
Communists had taken over the nationalism and where the
arrival of Caucasian soldiers might aid the enemy politi-

cally, but rather in terms of his own reckoning of the domino theory. "I am not going to be the President who saw Southeast Asia go the way China went," he said. In military terms, he saw the war not as an extension of the French war— what one reporter later described as dreaming different dreams than the French, but walking in the same footsteps —but as an extension of the Alamo. He told the National Security Council: "Hell, Vietnam is just like the Alamo. Hell, it's just like if you were down at that gate and you were surrounded and you damn well needed somebody. Well by God, I'm going to go—and I thank the Lord that I've got men who want to go with me, from McNamara right on down to the littlest private who's carrying a gun." Tom Wicker, of *The New York Times,* quotes Johnson talking about his Mexican neighbors in his excellent book on Johnson and Kennedy. "They'll come right in your yard and take it over if you let them. And the next day they'll be right on your porch barefoot, and weighing one hundred and thirty pounds, and they'll take that too. But if you say to 'em, 'hold on, wait just a minute,' they'll know they're dealing with someone who'll stand up. And after that, you can get along fine." "The enemy in Vietnam," noted Wicker, "was barefoot and weighed one hundred and thirty pounds. He was the kind of man who might be fine in his place, who could be a useful citizen and a good friend if he let you train him right and help him a little, but who would take over your front porch if you didn't stand up to him. Lyndon Johnson was not about to let little brown men who skulked in the jungle do that to him and the United States of America. . . ."

Badly advised by his immediate aides, most of whom were Kennedy men, Lyndon Johnson, who had helped deny John Foster Dulles the air strikes he had sought for Dienbienphu in 1954, now plunged the country into what would be a major, useless, tragic and divisive war. He did it with a totally unnecessary miscalculation of the nature of the war, of the enemy, and of his own popular mandate. He did it at a time when America's domestic problems were in desperate need of a solution, or at least the beginning of a solution. He listened to the military whom he had traditionally mistrusted, and who had already been proven consistently wrong on Vietnam. He had entered the office with an extraordinary mandate for social progress in America, intent on going down as a great president. Now the war was to destroy his presidency, destroy his hopes for social reform, cloud his chances for any serious historical recognition and, perhaps most bitter of all, the divisions and unrest the war was to create would rebound to the political advantage of the Democratic politician he disliked the most, Robert Kennedy. The Johnson years would look like a terrible Greek tragedy; both John Kennedy and Lyndon Johnson would have their Bays of Pigs—but one would last for several days and the other, for several years.

Normally this country supports its wars. They are not things to be sought after; but if unavoidable, and all other things being equal, the people will rally around—for a limited period of time, perhaps because this is a democracy —and give the administration the benefit of the doubt. But this war very quickly became different. Its historical roots were questionable; it was very far away and not noticeably connected to American security; it inflicted a particularly high price on noncombatants, something abhorrent to the American mind; and it had already been surrounded by a very considerable amount of disingenuousness. The more scrutiny the war received, the more the public would not like it. This was not because Americans were too soft and too unwilling to take on a difficult, complicated challenge, but because it was only with time that they would find the war not only untidy, but unworthy and unwinnable. And this, the long-range public distaste for the war, was, like the bogging down of American forces, entirely predictable.

Almost from the start the war was questioned. The major columnists of the country sensed that the more the country committed itself to Vietnam, the deeper it seemed to get, yet without getting any closer to victory. There was growing distrust of the President, who was, to use James Reston's phrase, escalating by stealth. Step by step the Americans were drawn in deeper and deeper. Now there were 500,000 in Vietnam, but even that many seemed to be sucked in by the lush countryside. The most powerful nation in the world, one which had brought tangible physical power to an awesome new degree, appeared to be using that power against a people who seemed, at best, to be mounted on water buffalo. Hawks and doves were named, and for a time it was fashionable to be a hawk. Hawks were tough and respectable; there was nothing queer about hawks. Doves were soft, dubious, perhaps unpatriotic; they might, under certain conditions, give away most of Southeast Asia. For a time doves would dress in hawks' clothing, keeping their dark secret as hidden as possible. But as the nation learned more and more about the war, the migration went in only one direction—from hawk to dove. The more that was perceived, the more respectable it became to be a dove. The real opposition began on the campuses. A new generation with a vast untapped political potential of its own felt particularly strongly about the war, and felt itself basically unrepresented in America. It had felt itself represented when Kennedy was alive; Johnson it regarded as much older, both because of years and because of style. As for the House of Representatives, it wrote it off as a citadel of old men in their fifties and sixties. This generation

was a potent political force; for a politician in his late
thirties or early forties not to deal with it, not to sense its
moods and priorities, would have been like a politician in
the late 1930s not taking into account the preferences of
blue-collar workers. Twelve and a half million Americans
had come of voting age since the 1964 election, and while
they would not be a lifetime political force for the Lyndon
Johnsons of America, they would for the Robert Kennedys
and John Lindsays—a politician who neglected them on
the war might never get them back. Political authorities
noting these statistics have always pointed out that traditionally the young do not vote; but, as Kennedy aide Fred
Dutton pointed out, the poor never voted either, until Roosevelt came along, and then they had a reason; and perhaps, in
1968, this would also be true of the young. (Not all politicians sensed this. Much later in the year a former Kennedy
man was called in by Humphrey to discuss ways in which he
might attract the youth. "Young people," said Humphrey,
"they don't vote." Yes, said his assistant Bill Connell, "all
they do is smoke pot.") To the young the war was regarded
as *their* work, the work of old men wallowing in the past,
repeating the old mistakes of American life. The college
students felt the war intensely; it was not a vague issue, but
indeed one that might take their lives. In home after home,
their influence on their parents would be spectacular—this
was to be one reason why the upper-middle class suburbs
would be so dovish in 1968.

There developed a certain rhythm to the opposition
to the war; it increased in multiples. The longer the war
went on, the more people learned about it, and the more
they were driven into opposition, thus encouraging others to
dissent. The longer the war went on, the more it was not
just a little war, but rather a war which began to dominate

American life. Men who had formerly kept their doubts private were now moved to express them. Now it was affecting not just the automatic doves, the people whose opposition was easily predictable, but more conservative establishment figures—men who watched carefully and were worried not so much about the war itself but about what it was doing to America. Gradually they came in; and as establishment figures came in, the opposition became more respectable, and thus even more doves surfaced. By 1967 the opposition to the war was at least as respectable as that in support of it, and it was growing all the time. The war was now backfiring; all the promises of Johnson and Westmoreland were being undermined daily. The doubters were beginning to look increasingly prophetic. Day by day, starting in late 1966, opposition to the war was becoming increasingly centralized; it was hard to gauge electorally, but it was there and growing.

The American public thinks of Lyndon Johnson as being too much of a politician. Poll after poll shows this, and as such the myth has grown that Johnson, whatever else, is a master politician. Curiously, Johnson is not a particularly good politician at all. He understands the Senate, how to maneuver and how to manipulate and overpower men there—how to deal with their weaknesses and strengths at close quarters—but he does not understand national politics, the delicate and complex balance of a country, particularly well. He tried to play Senate politics at the Democratic Convention in 1960, and was destroyed. Now in the White House he proved himself a bad politician again. He was unwilling to trust the public, but tried instead to outsmart it—in doing so, becoming increasingly a prisoner of his massive vanity. He was unable to confess error to a population remarkably tolerant of error, particularly if it is self-confessed. Of course a man who confesses to error is ipso facto not a politician; he is an honest man. The more opposition mounted, the more Johnson responded to it; but he responded with temporary measures: tricks, gimmicks, peace feelers, flying trips to Hawaii, trips to Vietnam, the bringing home of Westmoreland. Of course every time he did something, every time there was a trip or a gimmick, there would be a positive response—the nation would be pleased, the polls would show an increase in his popularity, and the doves would be on the defensive. But the war was not just a temporary thing. Though it was pleasant and colloquial to talk about bringing back coonskins, the war was, in reality, a cruel hopeless conflict which could not be won, which would not go away, and in which the balance had not been altered. Very powerful forces were at work there, and they would not be gimmicked. What Lyndon Johnson was doing all those years, starting in 1965, was buying time for his war; but again, he was doing so at the price of his own credibility, and again, it was a very high price indeed. Each time the cry against the war rose, he would fend off the critics, but he would use up a little more of his credibility. Thus he was buying temporary success but creating long-term problems. A smart politician doesn't do that. Instead, he suffers immediate problems and takes the long-range gain—he is willing to let the polls be low early in the administration if he is accruing gains which will help him at election time.

Moreover Lyndon Johnson was mistaken in his ideas about consensus opinion and his own position within the Democratic party. The consensus he was after was a national one, half Republican and half Democratic, but the dissent happened to be in the Democratic party which might block his chance to run again. One had only to look at the Senate Foreign Relations Committee, where almost all of the Democrats dissented and many of the Republicans assented, to understand the curious political split. Johnson was taking his own normal constituency for granted, counting on the traditional mythology, and concentrating instead on taking over what he believed was the middle. This might seem like a smart strategy, but in the process his natural base, the liberal wing of his own party—a faction of great influence and vocal power in this country—had almost completely turned on him. Thus the people who should have normally been most devotedly for him, willing to work for him, to contribute to his campaign, to publicize his many virtues, were most devotedly and passionately against him.

In this period of growing social and political dissatisfaction, the role of Robert Kennedy was crucial. He was at the exact median point of American idealism and American power. He understood the potency of America's idealism, as a domestic if not an international force, and yet he had also exercised American power. The correlation was such that his speeches could be written by young radicals like Adam Walinsky and Peter Edelman, and yet his children named after Douglas Dillon and Maxwell Taylor. Though Kennedy was part of the politics of the past, and had dealt skillfully, if at times somewhat roughly, with the old bosses, he understood the mandate of the new politics and the importance of keeping up with the kids. If he had been a partner, and for a long time an enthusiastic one, to early decisions in Vietnam, by the end of

his brother's presidency he had been one of the first to
sense that things were not working out. In 1968 reporters
traveling with him, or with one of his aides, like Kenny
O'Donnell, would hear again and again the lament about
those days: They kept promising us, they kept misleading
us. From the start Kennedy had doubted the validity of the
American commitment of combat troops, sensing that the
war was unwinnable. He went out of his way to keep himself
informed on Vietnam, talking to all the dissenters, to people
who had visited Hanoi. At a time when the administration
was carefully screening itself from any informed doubter,
making sure that no criticism reached the President's ears,
Kennedy was talking to all the people who were voicing
their private and public doubts about the war. He knew
also what the war was doing to the country, that it was
sharpening the existing divisions, making the thin fabric
which bound American life that much thinner.

Yet his position was particularly vulnerable. In a sense
there were not just two political parties in America in the
late sixties, but really three—the Democrats headed by
Johnson, the Republicans, and the Kennedys, almost a party
unto themselves. It was a government in exile with its own
shadow cabinet and with Robert Kennedy as the titular
head. Everything he did was viewed as part of his own
candidacy—every move, every motive was doubted; nothing
could be innocent. If he spoke out on Vietnam it would not
be judged as a statement by a concerned politician on a
crucial issue, but as an instance of petty political maneuver-
ing. Yet the other half of that coin was his power: dissent
by Robert Kennedy on the war was not idle dissent, it was
dissent by so powerful a political figure on so important an
issue as to represent a frontal challenge to the administration. With Robert Kennedy on their side the doves would

become that much more respectable. The Kennedys are not soft, they are tough; they are Irish; they are formidable practicing politicians, and one is not ashamed to have them as colleagues. Had any other politician in America spoken, as Robert Kennedy almost innocently had, of giving blood to the Vietcong, his career as a serious political figure would have been over; for Kennedy it was a temporary slip. If Robert Kennedy became a dove, a lot of other people, senators, writers and plain citizens, would feel more at ease in joining them; and those tenuously critical of the administration would be encouraged and strengthened, and they would become more sharply critical. The entire rhythm of protest would be accelerated that much more.

In early 1966 Robert Kennedy broke with the administration over Vietnam. There was no single clear point of demarcation, rather it was more a matter of tone and emphasis. He did not really attack the war or the President, he simply said that the emphasis of the war was wrong, that the administration was placing too much emphasis on military solutions as opposed to political solutions, perhaps a coalition, perhaps a bombing halt. It was not so much criticism as implied criticism; it was not so much an attack upon the administration as it was implied support of the dissenters. But both the administration and the dissenters knew where Kennedy was headed. If Lyndon Johnson had escalated the war by stealth, Robert Kennedy was becoming a dove by stealth—but his course was clear. In November 1966, right after the congressional elections, at a time when American political conversation turns inevitably to the next presidential election, a group of *Time* magazine writers assembled at dinner. One reporter, just back from Vietnam and knowledgeable about the war and the coming frustration there, predicted that Kennedy would run for the presidency in 1968—not because he wanted to, not because he

intended to, but because forces outside his control would
demand that he do so. The war could only get worse, and as
the war became worse the public malaise would grow, and
by March 1968, the crucial time—the time of the primaries
—the pressure on Kennedy as the leader of the opposition
would be unbearable. He would have to either run or surrender leadership. For that position was not just his alone,
the party at this particular time inevitably would have a
bright young man who would represent fresher ideas and a
rallying point. The Kennedy phenomenon had made the
Kennedys the controllers of that particular position, and
after the assassination it had fallen by succession to Robert
Kennedy. With their power and their ability to attract intellectuals the Kennedys so dominated the young leadership
of the party that anyone else virtually had to fall into their
orbit, clear it with them whether or not he ran. But that slot
which Robert Kennedy held as the youthful attractive figure
challenging the old order was one which would exist without him, it was a natural vacancy, not a man-made one—
and his control of it might be only temporary.

His dissent grew, and with it, the opposition to the war.
The White House predictions about imminent victory came
and went, developing a rhythm of their own. Optimism
about imminent victory was followed by a call for more
troops, which was followed by more optimism for a more
imminent victory. The ghettos became increasingly restless;
city after city burned. The unique ghetto was the one which
did not burn. As these forces mounted, Kennedy himself
became increasingly radical and listened more and more
to radical *social* voices. By early 1967 he was preparing to
make a major address on Vietnam—a real and serious break
with the administration which would become a watershed of
opposition. He traveled through Europe meeting heads of
state. In Paris he might even have been the recipient of a

peace feeler, though one never knew (peace feelers are where you find them, if you want to find them; there was a time in 1966 when the mayor of every city in every neutral country proclaimed that he had just received a peace feeler). Then he returned to Washington to meet with Johnson for a final break.

All the bitterness and acrimony between these two powerful men, perhaps the two most powerful men in the country—one with actual power, the other with potential power—surfaced at the meeting. Kennedy had never been generous with the President after his brother's assassination. He felt that Johnson was a usurper of his brother's office, and a destroyer of his brother's dream, the dream of all the fine young men. Now that dream was being betrayed, being dragged into a hopeless war. Johnson, proud and vain, nursed long-held antagonism for Robert Kennedy. Kennedy had not wanted him on the ticket in 1960; he had treated him with disdain for three years in office, and had then wanted to be Johnson's vice-president. Johnson felt that Kennedy had never forgiven him for his ascension, that he had behaved ungenerously to him—"All that boy has done since I became President," he told one friend, "is snipe at me. He's been running for office since I was sworn in." His feelings were sharpened by the ease with which Kennedy handled public relations, by the glamour which was attached to Kennedy and which eluded him, and he was particularly bitter about Vietnam. He felt he was carrying out the Kennedy mandate, using the Kennedy people, and now he was being politically attacked by the young man who started it. Robert Kennedy himself had said in 1962, in Saigon, "We are going to win and we are going to stay here until we win." The President was angry and bitter. He began the meeting by denouncing Kennedy for having made alleged peace-talk leaks.

Kennedy immediately replied that he had not leaked anything. "That came from your state department," he said.

"It's your state department," Johnson said angrily.

Then they began to argue bitterly. Kennedy, according to some reports, called the President a son of a bitch. Then Johnson began to talk about the war, to criticize Kennedy for running down his own country. He told Kennedy that he would soon be in serious political difficulty. "We are going to win this war, and in six months all of you doves will be politically dead." The President continued, in a line of argument he frequently used; the anger showed in his voice. Criticism by Kennedy and others encouraged Hanoi to hold on. Hanoi was tired and losing, but the doves kept alive their false hopes and kept the war from ending. The doves were prolonging the war. If you persist, he said, "the blood of American boys will be on your hands." He looked at Kennedy and told him, "I could attack you in exactly those words and if I do, you will be finished."

"I don't have to sit here and listen to this kind of talk," Kennedy said. The meeting broke up.

Less than a month later, after an enormous amount of advance build-up, Kennedy made his major Vietnam speech. The build-up had been immense, and for days reporters had been clamoring for leaks. Would he be hawk or would he be dove? "We'll send up puffs of white smoke if it's dovish, gray if it's hawkish," said Frank Mankiewicz, his press secretary. The decision, when it came, was a clear break with the administration. While admitting his own responsibility for past mistakes, he finally came out and attacked the war itself and U.S. responsibility for it. "It is *we* who live in abundance and send our young men to die. It is our chemicals that scorch children and our bombs which level villages. . . ." He called for a bombing pause and a coalition settlement supervised by the United Nations. Johnson was not amused. He gave two speeches that same day, and also announced that Russia had agreed to discuss the limiting of the missile race.

Thus Robert Kennedy broke with the administration and acceded to the titular leadership of not only the Kennedy party, but also of those who were now leading the dissent on Vietnam and were looking for strong political leadership. (Many of them had been formerly anti-Kennedy; barely reconstructed Stevensonians.) It was perhaps smart politics, but it was done, ironically, without any political stratagem in mind. In early 1967 it was quite clear that Kennedy had no intention of running for office—he did it because he could not do otherwise. Yet in accepting the leadership of the opposition, he accepted certain obligations too. He was leading on an issue of such gravity that it would not easily be postponed; it held that quality of moral imperative. But he had thought, in accepting this leadership, that though it might be distasteful he could wait five years, until 1972. Yet his troops were rallying to him, not just because he was a Kennedy or because they wanted a restoration, but because he looked like the only Democrat capable of beating Johnson in 1968.

But he was really thinking in terms of 1972; he was not planning on 1968. The long-range forces he had counted on, the young people voting in large numbers, the dominance of television, the liberation from the bosses, would come with the new politics in 1972. But because of Vietnam, 1968— the transitional year from new politics to old politics— beckoned; and he was there.

Robert Kennedy was in many ways the most interesting figure in American politics, not only because he was a

Kennedy, not only because so much of his education had taken place in the public eye—it could be traced by putting together film clips of this decade—but primarily because he was a transitional figure in a transitional year. At a time of great flux in American life and politics, with old laws on the way out and new laws on the way in, Robert Kennedy was at exactly the halfway mark between the old and new. His career spanned the old politics of the past, he had worked successfully in it, electing his brother President; and he now planned on success in the coming politics of the future, to elect himself President. Thus there was a constant struggle, for his body, his soul and his campaign, between the traditionalists, the veterans of 1960—most often John Kennedy men: Larry O'Brien, Ted Sorensen and others—and the new breed, most often young men, more radical, and less professional in the pure sense. They were Bob Kennedy men first and foremost, prophets of the new politics—men like Adam Walinsky, the young speech writer, and Frank Mankiewicz, the press secretary. Though in part a struggle in tactics, it was more: it reflected a collision of forces in America just as much as a decade ago a debate between liberals and conservatives in the Senate had reflected a similar collision. The result was that Robert Kennedy, just as he was caught in the great contradictions between the thrusts of American power and American idealism, was also caught in the contradictory thrusts of the new and the old politics. But he would be too tied to the past, surrounded by men who knew more of the past than of the future, and this would force him into a fatal mistake.

This year was a long way from 1960 and, for the first time since the New Deal, American politics were reflecting the major changes in American life. As such, the battle around Kennedy reflected shifts in the society. The old machine-based, party-centered, economics-oriented traditionalist politics were shifting, in our affluence, to new styles. New issues were surfacing, old alliances were breaking up, and new forces were coming into our politics. The party machinery, once the dominant force in the Democratic party, was steadily being weakened. There was a new middle class which was moving to the suburbs; if a family was already making $10,000, how could the machine offer a better job? There was also the onslaught of television which was wiping out the middleman, the power broker who, in return for certain promises and controls, could offer the candidate exposure. Now someone with money, or the ability to attract money, and the right personality, someone who could bear exposure, could go directly to the people. Political power, which once rested with party officials and labor unions, was shifting to the suburbs. Labor unions, threatened by the rise of the Negro, particularly in housing and employment, were fast becoming a conservative force. The easy old coalition between labor and Negroes was no longer so easy; it barely existed. The two were among the American forces most in conflict. Yet other groups, traditionally Republican, might now, in suburbia, be wooed to the cause.

Yet if part of the new politics worked, so did some of the old. The mix varied greatly from state to state and region to region, depending on the affluence of the area, on the population shifts, and on how much the area represented the business and style of the old America and how much it represented the drives and technology of the new. The electronics industry with its all-engineer suburbs was new America; the textile mills, old America. Some states, like California, were almost totally new politics; others, like Indiana, were curiously old politics, strikingly unchanged from their voter profile in 1960 or 1956, albeit a bit more affluent.

Thus the new politics was the sum of many changes.

Labor and labor districts though more affluent were not very
affluent, and their hold in the society was a somewhat
marginal and insecure one. They no longer responded automatically to machine or union control. They feared the
Negroes, and this undermined one part of the party's traditional base. Similarly however, in the suburbs a large portion
of middle-class America, nominally Republican, had been
freed from some of its economic fears. It had become ma-
terially successful, and now had time on its hands to worry
about the course of American life. Most often it is bothered
by moral issues. Its feeling on race is ambivalent. It does
not feel the thrust of the Negro and his anger the way the
blue-collar whites do. It would like to be for the Negro, and
yet it is uneasy about the new anger of American blacks; it
does not like anger or sweatiness on the part of anyone. In
a sense labor now resembles the middle-class Republican
America of thirty years ago. In the thirties, white-Protestant
small-town America was the heartland of America. It had
its share of the pie, but was worried about the upward push
of labor in the Democratic party: Would that diminish the
pie? Labor was the radical, on the outside trying to get in.
Now, those sons of businessmen, well trained in the new
technocratic America, have moved up. Very secure in their
jobs, they have learned that labor is no threat. But labor,
finally getting its share of the pie, is now uneasy about the
upward drive of the Negro. Is it a threat? Will it diminish
the piece of pie? Labor is on the inside these days, but without much security or generosity. George Wallace discovered
this in the early sixties. He had sensed the anger and frustration of the blue-collar people and the new class division in
American life; that the middle class was for the Negro but
had fled to the suburbs leaving behind an angry blue-collar
class to live next door to the Negroes. (In late July, 1968,
Wallace turned to a reporter and said, "You reporters are

for McCarthy, aren't you; and your editors are for Humphrey; *but your pressmen are for me.*") The new middle class had moved to the suburbs; it now had the time and energy to work in American politics. It was far removed from blind party loyalty, indeed it regarded party loyalty as just a little bit unsavory and almost dishonest; rather, it voted for the better man (as seen on television). Who got the suburbs, and could continually understand its needs, would most likely dominate the new politics.

Even the kids were different. They were largely middle class, affluent, not worried about their jobs—the jobs would always be there. They were a politically charged up generation, a product of stepped-up American education. They were in high school during the John Kennedy years; the civil-rights revolution was part of their times, it was a moral issue to them, and they were touched deeply by Vietnam. It was likely to be the most politically active generation in our history.

Technically, and Robert Kennedy understood this better than most people, the first year for the Democrats to operate under the new politics would be 1972. (Indeed his friend Fred Dutton had written a book on the new politics. It was to come out during the campaign and would warn Kennedy not to run until 1972; Dutton would have to revise the book under combat conditions.) The Republicans, less tied to the machine, would have a quicker shot at it if they chose the right candidate. If Kennedy himself was in a dilemma about his own decision, he seemed to view the opportunities of others much more clearly. Lindsay, he told one friend in January, was crazy not to go for it. It was wide open for him, and this was his year—just as 1960 had been Jack Kennedy's year. All it would take would be organization and audacity; the money and the talent would find the candidate once he announced. But the friend protested:

Lindsay was locked in by Rockefeller who had prior claim
to the same constituency. "If I were Lindsay," Kennedy said,
"I'd go to Rockefeller and I'd say, 'Governor, I admire you
and your record, and I think you're the man to lead the
liberals to victory this year. And we need the leadership,
and I want to be for you. But it's important that this time
we not be divided as before and that the liberals take the
leadership early. So I hope you'll announce. But if you don't
announce in three weeks, I'm going to announce myself.' He
could have gone all the way this year." By a hard-nosed
look, the thing for Robert Kennedy to do was to wait until
1972. But life was not like that; the forces brought to bear
by Vietnam were forcing him to make 1972 decisions at a
time when the structure was still old politics. Mayor Daley
of Chicago was still a powerful figure and there were other,
lesser, unsympathetic bosses to deal with. The moral forces
of the new politics were sweeping across the country in advance of the political realities of the new politics. Thus, a
terrible struggle for Kennedy.

It was a struggle which had begun as early as 1965,
when Kennedy was shaping his new direction and his own
staff—a surprisingly radical staff. He was gathering the
kind of men he would now listen to, and thus to a large
degree he was charting his own increasingly independent
course in politics. It was a struggle which would reach its
height, over whether or not Kennedy should run, in the late
fall of 1967, and winter of 1967 and 1968. It was a classic
struggle between the new politics people and the old pros.
On the one side there were the young radicals (of one very
young speech writer an older Kennedy aide said: "That kid
gets his draft notice and we're the only campaign in
town with a speech writer in Canada"), also people like

Mankiewicz who had come to Robert Kennedy rather than Jack Kennedy, and a few of the older eggheads, like Schlesinger and Galbraith. On the other side were the old pros, the 1960 veterans, including Larry O'Brien who held, at the time, that most radical of seats, Postmaster General under Lyndon Johnson.

As early as the fall of 1966, two of Kennedy's legislative aides had sensed the new currents, that the war would drag on and that the only new thing in the political equation of the war would be the growing national malaise. They saw Lyndon Johnson increasingly a prisoner of the war, and they believed that by 1968 the country would be ripe for a new, modern and *moral* candidacy. There would be new issues and a rejection of old foreign-policy clichés. More, they felt it should be a Kennedy candidacy. They felt a delicate and fragile balance would work for him in 1968. It would bloom once, and if he did not rise to it, it might never bloom again: for moral leadership once offered could not be easily postponed, it might pass to someone else. Walinsky and the others sensed that a Republican, Lindsay most likely, might easily move in and become the hero, if not winning, at least becoming the odds-on favorite for 1972. They did not figure on Eugene McCarthy.

Kennedy's staff was an interesting assortment. They were by and large Robert Kennedy men first, more than Jack Kennedy's, and attracted by what they saw as Robert Kennedy's instinct for radicalism. They would see the bumper stickers saying "Bobby Ain't Jack," and they would say to reporters: yes, that's true, but not in the way these people think. Jeff Greenfield kept copies of college editorials he had written attacking Jack Kennedy's Vietnam policies. There was a feeling among them that the early Kennedy years and the early Kennedy people were too cold-war oriented. Walinsky had joined Robert Kennedy after the State Department

had tried to block pacifist A. J. Muste's peace march from
Quebec to Guantanamo and Walinsky, a very young justice
department attorney, had prepared a memo denying State's
authority. Kennedy had backed Walinsky saying, "If an
eighty year old man wants to walk eight hundred miles I
don't think it endangers the country. . . ." Mankiewicz, a
peace corps official, had been drawn to Kennedy during a
briefing in late 1965. The Senator was about to embark on a
major trip through Latin America and he met with high
State Department officials. Kennedy had asked what he
should say about the Dominican Republic intervention, and
Jack Hood Vaughn, then Assistant Secretary of State for
Latin American affairs, had said, "You could tell them what
your brother said at the time of Cuba." The ice began to form
and Kennedy said, "I hope you're not going around quoting
President Kennedy to defend the Dominican Republic." It got
worse from then on, Vaughn telling Kennedy not to worry
because no one in Latin America cared about the Dominican
events anyway. Kennedy asked what he should say in Brazil,
and Vaughn suggested he say nothing, that's what the
Latins usually do. They discussed problems of American
oil companies in Peru—the government had moved against
these companies and this had triggered a cutback in aid.
Finally Kennedy looked at Vaughn and said, "Well Mr.
Vaughn, the way you state it, the Alliance for Progress has
come down to this: you can suspend the constitution and
dissolve your political parties and exile your opposition and
you'll continue to get all the aid you want, but if you play
around with an oil company, it's cut off." There was no
reply; it was very tense. At the meeting Mankiewicz, bitter
about American policy in Latin America, had been the only
official to speak out critically on American policies. The next
day he breakfasted with Kennedy, and a few months later,
faced with the prospect of leaving Washington, he went to

work for Kennedy as a press secretary. These men pushed hard for a race, along with others such as Lowenstein who intended to have a candidate come hell or high water.

But the traditionalists had argued against it, men like Ted Sorensen, O'Brien. Amateurs willing to take risks in 1960, they had become professionals, establishment figures, by 1967 (witness Sorensen representing General Motors against Ralph Nader). The 1960 John Kennedy campaign had never been run outside the political establishment: it had been run to prove to the Democratic political apparatus, much of it Catholic and thus terribly sensitive on the issue, that a handsome young Catholic could win. However, they were now, in 1967, passing on the same clichés of American politics. The same men who had scoffed in 1960 when someone said a Catholic could not win, not yet anyway, were now saying yes, but you can't unseat a sitting president. They were wealthy and successful men now. They had important jobs which placed them in contact with powerful, wealthy men, and simultaneously removed them from the new forces now being generated in American politics. Sorensen seemed symbolic: heralded in the press as a great liberal who had taught Jack Kennedy his liberalism, and had masterminded the great victory, he had gained an insider's reputation, during the White House years, of being the most pragmatic politician of all, far removed from his liberalism. Following the assassination he did not plunge himself into the social issues with which the administration had been so concerned, but rather became just one more wealthy lawyer. Had he spent those post-assassination years working in ghettos or with Negroes, he might have felt the moral intensity of the times and he might have been more in touch with the country. Later in 1967 and 1968 his various public statements on the campaign sounded, ideologically, like those of someone from the Hubert Humphrey camp who had wandered into the Kennedy camp by mistake. (After the assassination he would talk publicly as though he had the right to barter the Kennedy mantle to Humphrey in exchange for some concessions on Vietnam.) His was in all a curious performance; and he had vigorously opposed Kennedy's making the race. Symbolically, of all the old Kennedy people who got together at a Kennedy meeting in December, 1967, the one most sympathetic to the race was Kenny O'Donnell. He was not yet for Kennedy's making it, but very close to it ("I'm almost there now," he said at the time). He was in Massachusetts and could feel directly the first pressure of the college kids going for McCarthy; feel the potency of the new force, and feel it slip away from the Kennedys.

The traditionalists passed on the myth that the country was more hawkish than you thought, which was not true. The country was less hawkish than you thought. The move was from hawk to dove and fast, and the polls which they carried to the meeting and quoted were wrong for two reasons: first because people do not tell pollsters the truth about how they feel if somehow they think it might mark them as unpatriotic, so that there is a very considerable built-in error; and secondly, and perhaps more important, because the questions were badly posed, and certainly not posed the way they would be in a vigorous and intelligent political campaign. Do you favor the war, are you against it, do you want to win, do you want to lose, do you want to escalate, or de-escalate. (Do you want to take a free trip around the world, all expenses paid, with a week with Brigitte Bardot in Paris. Do you want to take the same free trip around the world, all expenses paid, with the same week in Paris and the same week with Brigitte if it is going to give you terminal cancer?)

Another reason why the traditionalists counseled the conventional wisdom was that they had served in the presidency and seen the wide and extraordinary range of its powers. (Indeed they were not the only people who believed that you could not unseat a sitting president. The airlines thought so too. American Airlines which, like TWA, wanted domestic routes, would offer a 727 to the Kennedys at the start of the campaign for a rough rental of about $130,000 a month; after Johnson withdrew the price suddenly came down to about $30,000. The price for an Electra, roughly $70,000 a month while Johnson was still a candidate, dropped to $18,000. It was a quick study in presidential power.) These 1960 men had become traditional professional politicians, and to challenge the traditional laws was to challenge their own being. They had, after all, a candidate who might easily become president of the United States if he waited, and as such they felt they had something to lose. They had become conservative low-risk politicians. Some of them, like Pierre Salinger, a little lazy, a little arrogant, had said too many silly things about Vietnam. (After Kennedy finally went in he ran into Salinger and teased him about this. "Are you a hawk or a dove now, Pierre?" he asked. Salinger answered, quickly and seriously, "Oh-I'm-a-dove-now-I'm-a-dove-now.") Also, and this was crucial, there were basically differing views of Vietnam and the nation. After Kennedy made his major speech on Vietnam, in early 1967, he turned to Edelman, one of the young radicals, and asked, "Am I a big enough dove for you now, Peter?" No, said Edelman. "Good," said the Senator, "that makes me feel a little better." But of that same speech Sorensen would tell Jimmy Breslin that it was a mistake "because Bob Kennedy is the only hope in this country for your children and my children. And we can't afford to have him in controversies this early."

Kennedy's own instincts were probably to run. His

wife Ethel badly wanted him to. She sensed his moral commitment, and she sensed that he would be miserable and
never forgive himself if he didn't go. Kennedy sensed the
changes. But if he had the advantages of the past, the name,
the ability to assemble bright young men, the ability to
make headlines, he also had the liabilities of the past. He
was surrounded by advisers who had aged, and he was
particularly vulnerable to them. They had been advisers,
intellectual advisers, to Jack Kennedy, and that was part
of his blind spot. That meant they were automatically superior, perhaps more intellectual than he was. He had not
realized that in the restless chase of the last four years he
had gone beyond them; he now knew more about the country
and its mood than they did. He did not trust his instincts,
and it was a crucial mistake.

Gene McCarthy, not tied to the past, able to accept the
issue on its moral value alone, went in. It seemed at the
beginning a particularly frail candidacy. As late as Febru-
ary 3, the Gallup poll would show President Johnson's national margin over McCarthy to be 71 percent to 18, with 11
undecided. McCarthy's campaign seemed to lack the
glamour, the drive, *charisma,* one expected in a national
campaign. (Everyone expected a candidate to have charisma. Even Pat Paulsen, the Smothers Brothers' presidential
candidate, was once asked: "Mr. Paulsen, do you have charisma?" "No," he answered, "I had it once in the Marine
Corps but I haven't had any since.") McCarthy was seen,
after having announced for the presidency, eating alone in
restaurants in Washington and New York. His scheduling
was bad. Hours and hours of his prime time seemed to be
wasted. His meetings were often only half filled. The campaign was run on a low key from the start, and, as it turned

out later, a deliberately low key. Some of his closest aides and backers were worried from the start. They thought low key was all right, but there was a point where it bordered on laziness, and they sometimes wondered whether there was something physically ailing the candidate, something he had not told them about.

Sometimes McCarthy seemed to mock the entire process—laughing at the system, laughing at the traditional rites of vote-seeking, even mocking himself. If he had to give good lines, if he couldn't help being witty, then at least he could throw them away. Mary McGrory, a columnist who loved McCarthy, wrote that he was trying to run for the presidency without raising his voice. There was something unbending in him, a furious pride, and so at a time when he was doing something which genuinely dazzled the entire American intellectual establishment, when he probably could have had the best advisers and speech writers in the country, he had very few. His staff was often shockingly weak. He could not bear to solicit their aid, they had to volunteer it. And even then, when they did, it did not work well. He did not take well to other men's advice, nor did he use their ideas. This was a sharp contrast to the Kennedys who have always had an extraordinary ability to attract intellectuals and to retain them; to use just enough of their material to keep them committed, to make them feel they are making the breakthrough, winning the candidate to their view. McCarthy was also unlike Humphrey who has always been weak with intellectuals, unable to hold onto them because with all his energy he seemed anxious to prove that he didn't need them, he could do it all himself, thus leaving them unfulfilled.

McCarthy did not go through the usual pretensions either. He did not like the press and would not do the little things which made the daily life of reporters easier and endeared a candidate to them. He did not give them fire and, worst of all, he did not seem like a man running for the presidency. It all seemed terribly small-time. I remember trying to call Blair Clark, McCarthy's campaign manager, in early December after he announced. There was no campaign manager home; no answering service; it was only after many tries that a Negro maid answered. I gave my name, sensing, even as I did, that it would never reach Clark (it did not). One recalled McCarthy early in December at a meeting before a temple in Great Neck, Long Island. A long day for McCarthy: first a speech, then a press conference, the candidate patiently answering question after question for the television people. Finally he thought he was finished. "Now can we have a press conference for the writing reporters?" someone asked.

"I thought we just had one," McCarthy said.

"No you've had two conferences and both were for television. Now we can get serious?" the reporter asked.

McCarthy protested again: Look, he pointed to some reporters, they had asked questions and he had answered them, ergo a press conference. "I thought it was a press conference," he repeated.

"You've got a lot to learn," said the reporter.

"Yes," said McCarthy, "I have a lot to learn."

It was to get worse. The press would consistently underestimate his chances and, in McCarthy's view, underplay his activities; and he would grow embittered and occasionally petulant. He knew what they wanted him to do and say; he just as obstinately refused to do it. If they wanted anger, he would give them calmness. He would deliberately keep them waiting, often argue with them. A well-known columnist once asked for a copy of his speech. "What do you care?" McCarthy asked back, "You've never accurately reported my speeches before." Once he let the

reporters sit around waiting in a lobby for hours. When
they finally sent an aide up to see him, to express their dis-
pleasure, he snapped, "Why don't you go down there and
play them some music." To the mighty Walter Cronkite, interviewing him, he would point out that young David Schou-
macher, the regular CBS man and a favorite of his, asked
better questions. He was bitter toward the press. One sensed
that many of the frustrations he felt about American society
were symbolized by his dislike for the press; he felt he wasn't
demagogic enough for the American press. He felt they did
not give him credit for his intellectual superiority, they
wanted showmanship and they did not understand how he
was handling this particular issue. The press did underestimate him. Reporters would see him ambling through
his schedule in New Hampshire, giving what were pre-
dominantly bad speeches. The first three times I heard him
he was simply terrible, giving his regular lecture-circuit
$1,000-special on the History of Humanitarian Thought in
the West. Stevenson without Stevenson, I decided. The reporters did not believe his own explanation—that the issue
was already too emotional; it was there, deep in the people
themselves, and all they needed was a political outlet for it
and that was what he was providing. He was playing it very
well, the quiet man. He had felt the mood; he had decided
that the people felt there was already too much divisiveness
in the country. His style was not to be divisive. He came
across well in some of those small meetings. They listened
and decided that yes, Gene McCarthy is a gentleman.

More, he had a cool analytical eye and he realized,
himself, that American politics were changing and changing
quickly. Sometimes it seemed he could analyze better than
he could campaign. He sensed very early the new power of
the kids, the massive influence of television (whose reporters he treated better than writing reporters) and, more im-

portant, he sensed that simply by running he would get his
share of television time. He saw early that the old liberalism
was increasingly irrelevant, and that the old coalition was
fractured and by and large meaningless. The old liberals, he
said, would speak with pride on how hard they had fought
and were still fighting to pass civil-rights legislation, but
that much of this was now viewed as irrelevant. "Johnson,"
he told me in December while campaigning, "is going out
with a list of achievements, the laundry list, all these bills
he's passed, all these things he's done. What he doesn't
realize is that the people he's trying to convince don't care:
he hasn't answered the questions that bother them. It's become a moral question, a question of values. He hasn't got
their answers." He was articulating new issues and new
priorities for an affluent America, shifting the issues of the
Democratic party from the old economic orientation to new
moral ones, asking what the quality of American life would
be and what the thrust of American life would be. He was
saying, in effect, that the more traditional liberalism of the
last decade had failed because, though liberal legislation
had been passed, the immense burden of America's military
budget and foreign aid commitments had made the victories
meaningless and left social programs more bankrupt than
the nation realized. He was in this sense setting forth and
clarifying the issues, not just for this campaign but for the
next decade.

The New Hampshire campaign in early December was
pieced together almost against McCarthy's will. His advisers tried to tell him that running for president was different from running for the Senate, that it was not a small,
closed operation, that he needed the national press, and
most of all that he had to enter New Hampshire. McCarthy

did not want to enter. On that particular trip he wanted to tell all those nice, sincere, decent doves that he liked them and shared their idealism, but that he did not like their state; it had too many mountains, too few Democrats and too many hawks for his taste. One sensed that he was thinking about it—the long campaign ahead, all the snow, all the sore throats he would get. Just twenty-one days was all it would take, his New Hampshire people pleaded, just twenty-one days. They were the best people he had, and their quality of backbiting was surprisingly low for such good liberals; but he shook his head. All right they said, just fourteen days. Give us fourteen days in New Hampshire. Advisers like Lowenstein were arguing that if he went after the presidency, he had to go after each primary, he could not afford to be frightened away. A victory in a so-called dovish state such as Wisconsin would not be a victory unless he had also done well in so-called hawkish states. So he ambled, almost bumbling, through New Hampshire, appearing at meetings which were sometimes painfully small, talking about the need for changes in American life in a typically McCarthy style: "In the past, when a country won a war the successful leaders always stayed on one generation too long, but now, after World War II, with the invention of penicillin they have stayed on two generations too long, and that's the trouble with most of the world."

But the army of students was there too. It had been organized for more than a year, primarily by Lowenstein and a few sub-Lowensteins who traveled all over the country, telling the students that their dissent was not unique and that there would be an outlet this year. Lowenstein had alternated between the Reform Democratic clubs and the students—mixing in both, always late, always disorganized, and yet touching thousands of people. I remember one evening late in the spring of 1967 at Lowenstein's apartment. What, you've never met Norman Thomas? You've got to come by the house tomorrow night. And so I went, the next evening, to meet Norman Thomas. It was an extraordinary evening: Norman Thomas, almost blind now, Frank Graham, the former Senator from North Carolina who was successfully red-baited years ago, Mrs. Lowenstein, quite pregnant and quite confused—wondering who all these people were—and about twenty students, but no Lowenstein—he was circling above LaGuardia, in from another college visit. Some of the students were New Left, some of them very angry and bitter about the country and the war. Three very radical ones were arguing furiously with Thomas, saying that the war was racial and genocidal, white men deliberately killing yellow men. Thomas, turning with the sound, barely able to see, argued patiently that no, it wasn't a racial war, this country made a mistake. There was just too much American vanity and it was getting us in deeper. This was the radical Norman Thomas, my father's hero? Many of the people in charge, he was saying, feel about Negroes the same way you do. These generals, a girl shrieked, those generals feel anything about Negroes? Yes, said Mr. Thomas. Vintage stuff. Eventually Lowenstein arrived and packed everyone off to a West Side reform club meeting where he spent half the night attacking Johnson and the war, saying Johnson will be beaten, the politicians are wrong, it is in the air. Volunteers were asked for, and a few appeared.

These were bad days for Robert Kennedy. He was playing Hamlet—thinking about the race constantly, wanting to make it, being led there by his emotions again and again, only to be brought back from the brink by the cold words of his closest advisers. His position was terribly ambivalent. He had chartered an entire political course only to halt at its most crucial moment. He was still telling people that he would support Johnson for the presidency. He had failed to come out for McCarthy (if he were going to come out for McCarthy, he might as well come out for himself). Columnist Murray Kempton who had frequently penned love notes to Kennedy in the past, and who felt deeply for him, was writing bitterly in early January: "As of now I prefer Eugene McCarthy as a candidate for President of the United States. An obvious reason is that McCarthy has the guts to go. A less obvious but more significant reason is that I was not at all surprised that he would, and I'm not the least surprised that Kennedy wouldn't."

But it was the cartoonist Jules Feiffer with his fine eye for our contemporary foibles who caught the failure of Kennedy the best. In a cartoon strip entitled "The Bobby Twins," Feiffer portrayed a television debate between the Good Bobby and the Bad Bobby:

> *The Good Bobby:* We're going in there and we're killing South Vietnamese. We're killing children, we're killing women. . . .

> *The Good Bobby:* We're killing innocent people because we don't want to have the war fought on American soil.

> *The Good Bobby:* Do we have that right, here in the United States, to perform these acts because we want to protect ourselves?

> *The Good Bobby:* I very seriously question whether we have that right.

> *The Good Bobby:* All of us should examine our own consciences on what we are doing in South Vietnam.

> *The Bad Bobby:* I will back the Democratic candidate in 1968. I expect that will be President Johnson.

The Good Bobby: I think we're going to have a difficult time explaining this to ourselves.

But by late January it was no longer just a trickle of volunteers. In Cambridge, where feeling runs particularly strongly against the war, it was the minority which was *not* opposed and which was not activist. And so now, gathering from every state, the army marched on New Hampshire. Not everyone, it seemed, had completely turned off the system. These kids were quite obviously the best of a generation. Kennedy would later note ruefully that he had the B and B-minus kids and McCarthy had the A kids. Most of them were upper-middle class. Many of them were the sons and daughters of those who voted for Richard Nixon in 1960, who felt more at ease with Nelson Rockefeller than anyone else. The kids were at ease convincing the Hampshiremen that the war was an immoral cause; they had all practiced on their parents before.

Among the Jewish students there is something striking, the new security of American life. They are the sons of the affluent Jews in the suburbs, but they look more like their immigrant grandfathers, those radical Socialists from the old world with their beards. They were men who never felt shame about their political feelings, not at all like the next generation which wanted so desperately to be Americanized, which shaved its beards and out-WASP-ed the WASPs politically. No, these kids are much more secure in American life, and they seem almost to have their grandfathers' political views in a contemporary setting. They are all part of an affluent new society with jobs secure and waiting after college. Material security is part of their birthright. Their worries are different than their parents' were. They now worry about what kind of a country they live in, and they worry about the morality of American life and its affluence.

These volunteers are not interested in the great battles of their parents' day, the Depression and How It Was Solved by Franklin Roosevelt and Us. They are more interested in the moral thrust of America. They see not so much what has been done, as what has not been done. They do not doubt that capitalism, as a material system, works much better than communism, but they wonder openly about the use of its affluence. They are bored with the anti-communism of their parents and of most of the national journals, so bored, in fact, that any new youth-oriented publication, like *Ramparts*, gets the benefit of the doubt (just as the Communists get the benefit of the doubt), precisely because it is anti-Establishment, precisely because it is different; thus it is theirs. But in New Hampshire these kids were on their best behavior. They had found a tangible cause into which they could channel all that energy and frustration, and they did. They were intense, believing in their cause with a ferocity unmatched in contemporary politics. Many of the young men had been drawn from the brink of draft-card burning. Dan Dodd, a young student up from the Union Theological Seminary, told a reporter, "I was thinking of turning in my draft card but then the campaign began. We're not going to build grass-roots politics in time to end the war by November, but if we can end the present President's career, maybe we can do it by then." They were even willing to use a little cosmetology in order to help McCarthy; the girls' skirts became a little longer, beards were shaved off or, if not, were confined to manning the phones at headquarters. A note stuck on one of the bulletin boards there, just before the primary, read: "Over 40 percent we go on to Wisconsin; 30 percent back to school; 20 percent we burn our draft cards; 10 percent we leave the country."

They were carefully rehearsed in how not to offend the Hampshiremen; just how hard to push the issues;

and how to test for the extent of hawkishness, to sense whether it is fragile and can be turned around, or whether it is deep and hard-core and not worth the effort. The volunteers became overnight a very effective force; young, intelligent, very attractive, and surprisingly well-organized. They made a formidable impression in New Hampshire. They had intense devotion to cause and intense belief in themselves, and watching them, I realized something about the McCarthy campaign which was to recur again and again in the months to come: when people cheered McCarthy, they were cheering themselves.

Now too, in early January, there was money available. The big New York money, which traditionally has supported reform candidates—Kefauver, Stevenson, Humphrey, Javits—was beginning to go for McCarthy. But slowly, not in one great outpouring. These people were worried about the war, worried about the ghettos, and worried about the gold outflow, yet they were a little wary. They were tough-minded, and they weren't sure that their tiger was a real tiger; he looked a little soft. But Galbraith and others would argue their doubts away, and gradually the money came in. If it was coming in to McCarthy, then it was also not coming in to Lyndon Johnson. This was one more sign that he was in serious trouble—sitting President or not, he would need money and he would need active volunteers, and his chances of getting them were diminishing every day. Politically too, he was paying a price for the increasing isolation of the White House. If the country had paid a price in the exodus of talented men from the White House because of Vietnam, so had the administration. Now, strikingly without talent, it faced a national election.

Johnson has always had a problem with talented people, he has always had a reputation for mishandling and abusing staff, almost trying to humiliate and destroy the

men around him. With Vietnam, the situation was worse
than ever. Moyers, the brightest of Johnson's own people,
was gone, and to a degree, Johnson was unprepared for
national elections. In 1964 he had been aided by a number
of Kennedy people whose loyalty in that year was not in
doubt. But now it was different. He had Larry O'Brien, a
highly knowledgeable technician whom he had carefully
weaned away from the Kennedys. He had prevented him
from resigning along with all the other Irish Mafia by an
offer of the postmaster generalship. Robert Kennedy understood this; he told a friend he knew what it meant for a boy
who had been as poor as Larry O'Brien to sit in the Cabinet
of the United States. Kenny O'Donnell in particular was
bitter about O'Brien because they had agreed, together with
Dave Powers, to resign ensemble, and then O'Brien had
stayed on. In 1968, when O'Brien came back to the fold, he
and O'Donnell would, in a friend's words, "communicate but
not speak to each other." But Kennedy had been too understanding of the dilemma. O'Brien had never broken ties
with him, though the ties were strained at times, and now,
in early 1968, Johnson was uneasy. He did not trust O'Brien
and this proved costly, for O'Brien had an unusual knowledge of New Hampshire and the technology of its politics.
He had run Jack Kennedy's campaign there in 1960, and he
knew its balance. He could have helped, if nothing else, to
minimize mistakes. And there were incredible mistakes. The
Johnson operatives, for reasons known only to themselves,
allowed forty-five candidates to run in the President's name
for twenty-four convention slots, thereby splitting up the
vote and allowing McCarthy to get twenty of the delegates.
But Johnson was never sure of O'Brien; he did not entirely
trust him, and so he used Marvin Watson.

Marvin Watson symbolized in many ways the White
House at its lowest ebb in 1968; he was the loyalty officer of

the administration at a time when loyalty was becoming the transcending quality. Marvin Watson was known best to America as the man who wanted to monitor all the calls going in and out of the White House, and now he was the White House's political man. The campaign was disastrously run. McCarthy was smeared repeatedly as the agent of Hanoi. Governor John King said that any vote for McCarthy would be greeted "with cheers in Hanoi." Senator Thomas McIntyre said McCarthy would honor "draft dodgers and deserters." Radio spots attacked the "peace-at-any-price fuzzy thinkers who say 'Give up the goal, burn your draft card and surrender!'" But McCarthy, running quietly with his own special dignity, did not look like the candidate of Hanoi. The Johnson people were too dependent on the state machine. They had nearly all the local politicians, which made them look, particularly in their own eyes, unbeatable. They would be able to gather all the politicians at the top —men who were seemingly reflectors of what was going on underneath—and believed this meant they would carry the workers and small farmers. The White House felt, looking at these politicians, that there was no coercion in their support, though of course it was not overt, it was covert: McCarthy had looked like a long shot and the President, a sure shot. Besides, the role of a state organization is almost always overemphasized by politicians themselves, and political reporters. Because the machine dominates politics in the off season, it becomes the initial point of reference; politicians make their living at it, therefore they are presumed to know what is going on. The truth is that in a statewide gubernatorial election, a moderately well-run machine can function, can effect a certain limited percentage of votes, because it is dealing with jobs and the families of job holders; but the very same machine trying for a Senate race often blunders badly because patronage is not at stake and because there are other more important issues. And in New Hampshire, in 1968, there was a very basic issue: the war.

In January 1968, General Vo Nguyen Giap changed his strategy. Up until then the Vietnamese Communists, fighting their particular guerrilla war, had never made their challenge in the cities. It had always been in the rural areas, where the guerrillas could slip away using the natural resources of the land. As such, the toughness and resiliency of the enemy had never come across clearly to the American public. By the time television cameramen arrived the enemy would be gone; besides, the places were almost always nameless spots. But in January, General Giap launched the Tet offensive. Suddenly, it became painfully clear to the American public that the war was not going well; that the enemy was resilient and very tough; that most of the pacification work had been shattered; that we could barely protect Saigon; and that the predictions of the American leadership had been totally false. Up until then Lyndon Johnson had believed that the war was going well; perhaps not as well as some of the generals said, but well nonetheless. He believed that dissent was largely the work of a few east-coast intellectuals and professors, and that it would be rejected by the rest of the country, which was soundly patriotic. Now, day by day, as the nation watched the endless battles on its television sets, and read the discouraging accounts from Saigon, Johnson was becoming more and more a hollow man. He had staked his entire political future on the war. He had slowly used up his credibility; now it was gone. Now it was too late to bring General Westmoreland home again to address joint session. And for Lyndon Johnson it was worse than for most leaders, for he was not a lovable man. He did not generate charisma, had no popularity; he was the kind of man who needed tangible success to hold his troops in line, and now even that success eluded him.

When Robert Kennedy decided in December to stay out, the debate within his circle had not ended. If anything it had accelerated. Walinsky, the house radical (when on the road, during the campaign, friends would put signs on his office door: "Gone To Peking, back in two weeks." or "In Hanoi"), wanted to quit. It took great effort on the part of his friends to keep him on the staff, to keep him from resigning. Now he and others were warning the Senator of something Kennedy knew himself, that Robert Kennedy was becoming an old politician overnight, long hair or no. If it were true that in the new politics with the old broker out, a candidate could be created overnight, then it was also true that it was a fragile thing and could fade just as quickly.

He became restless again and he wanted to run. Two weeks before the New Hampshire primary he began to call friends regularly, asking their advice, hoping, said one friend, to hear them change their minds and tell him to go for it. He went regularly to colleges, knowing that he would be harassed and booed, that the disparity between what he had pledged to America and what he was doing would be challenged. It was almost a form of masochism; he sought their anger. Indeed when it was not there, when they did not challenge him, he was angry at their complacency and he would challenge them: how can you be so complacent when there is a war on and your contemporaries are dying?

He felt it all slipping away from him, and felt himself caught in the particular bind of 1968. Lowenstein remembers calling him about ten days before the New Hampshire primary, jubilant because it had begun to turn; it was all falling into place. "We're going to do it! We're going to do it!

It's the beginning of the end for Johnson," he said excitedly into the phone. "I expected the same enthusiasm at the other end, I was so carried away by what we were doing. But he was very cool, very restrained, and he said 'You don't think you're being too optimistic?' and then I realized how painful it must have been for him." Other friends called and told him that New Hampshire was going to break it open. They pleaded with him to make a tentative announcement; to say that he was thinking of entering, so that he could share in the vote, and so that he would not be accused of moving in on McCarthy's triumph after the primary. And in the last few days he began to move. Jesse Unruh, one of the powers in the Democratic party who had previously told him not to run, flew in from California with a poll which showed Kennedy beating Johnson roughly two to one, with McCarthy a distant third. This was crucial, for Unruh was the first of the Democratic party powers to favor the race. Up until then it had been nothing but eggheads and moralists, and when they would outline all the reasons for making the race, a Kennedy aide would say, "yes, I agree with all that, but how many delegates do you yourself have?" The Sunday before the primary Kennedy called his wife from the west coast and asked her to call Schlesinger and Galbraith and have them tell McCarthy that he was going in, a task that neither relished. Similarly Teddy Kennedy contacted Dick Goodwin, a Kennedy man now working for McCarthy in New Hampshire, and Goodwin passed along the word that Kennedy was considering coming in.

Then came the New Hampshire results; they were staggering to the outside world. As late as early March, a sampling made for *Time* magazine by Roper Associates gave Johnson 62 percent and McCarthy 11 percent. But McCarthy had polled a startling 42.2 percent of the Democratic vote to Johnson's 49.4. In addition, and this was to become a consistent factor, McCarthy ran very well among Republicans; with nothing but write-ins, he ran third on the Republican ticket, and he trailed the President by only 230 in overall votes; 29,021 to 28,791. It was a staggering victory for a country which was unprepared for it and yet delighted by it. There was one last meeting of all the Kennedy brass. Steve Smith, his brother-in-law, had formerly opposed the race, but was now for it: if it's in your blood, do it, he told the Senator. Most of the others were for it now. Burke Marshall, a trusted aide, was also for it, though cold logic was still against it. Two men still opposed it. One was Edward Kennedy, a traditionalist, highly structured, very good at working with delegates, reassuring them; a different kind of man from Robert, less committed to lost causes, and more at ease in the camaraderie of the Senate. The other, Ted Sorensen, still conservative and cautious, still waiting for 1972; arguing not the new politics but the old mathematics, pointing out that even if Robert won all the primaries he would still need three-quarters of all the delegates outside the South. Others, such as Schlesinger, who had earlier argued for the race, now told Kennedy to wait a little, not to rob McCarthy of his hour of glory, not to re-create the old fears and suspicions in the process. Some argued that he let McCarthy do the primaries and then move in; others argued that he wait, create an artificial draft by having people troop in to see him daily, pleading with him to run, and having the pleas carefully leaked to the papers, until finally, against all his better judgment, for love of country he would run. But Kennedy was a curiously unsubtle man, not given to political pantomime. And he blundered right in, gracelessly, unable to wait, seeming to deprive McCarthy of his sweetest hour. "He didn't even give us 24 hours so we could raise the money to pay our bills," one McCarthy kid told Mary McGrory. New issues were made, the old Bobby was temporarily re-created, and McCarthy, who had privately acted ungenerously to Kennedy in the weeks before and who was very chilly about the news that Kennedy was coming in, was handed the white-knight issue. He became Clean Gene. "Kennedy thinks that American youth belongs to him at the bequest of his brother," wrote Mary McGrory. "Seeing the romance flower between them and McCarthy, he moved with the ruthlessness of a Victorian father whose daughter has fallen in love with a dustman." But he was in nonetheless, and alive; pleased to be liberated from the indecision, pleased to be back out campaigning again. In the same Senate caucus room where John Kennedy had made his announcement eight years earlier, Robert Kennedy made his entry statement. Many of the old guard were there. Men like Pierre Salinger who wandered about patting people on the back and saying "just like old times." But he was wrong, it was not like old times. The candidate was different and, most important, the country was different.

II

Suddenly then, in the early spring, Robert Kennedy was running. A shy, abrupt and sometimes passionate man ("He's unassimilated, isn't he?" Robert Lowell once said, after watching him at a party), he was more at ease running his brother for president than running himself. Now devoid of his privacy, forcibly shorn of his shyness, he was trying to control some of his passion. The spot was hardly ideal. In the normally alien state of Indiana, he was campaigning in cities and villages, trying even the tiny hamlets; stopping at little crossroads where no candidate for president had ever been because it was part of the American ethic that the rich may run for office so long as they campaign harder and longer than the poor. He was campaigning among the black and white, though rarely among the black and white together, not in the America of the sixties. These were uneasy days in an uneasy territory, for he was marked, this Irish son of an Irish millionaire, as being not just the friend of the black (indeed practically the black candidate) but Catholic as well. This was hostile soil, a land which had given Richard Nixon, though in 1968 it was hard to believe, 225,000 more votes; and there to remind him of both the past and the present were the bumper stickers, "Nixon Is Safer." When they said safer, they meant, and everyone knew it, Kennedy is Unsafe. (Nixon memorabilia amused Kennedy, particularly a signboard which showed Nixon, trustworthy, healthy, sober, carrying a briefcase, and doing something sound and practical for his country, and said: "Nixon is the One." He would tease with the crowd. "Nixon's the one *what*? ... Look at that briefcase. ... I've been wondering all this time what's in that briefcase. ... Do you think he's a briefcase salesman?")

Robert Kennedy's aides were masters at bringing him to the right places, big cities for big Democratic votes, so that over the television screens that night there would be flashed photographs of huge crowds mauling Robert Kennedy, and a message to be read by the bosses of the Democratic party. But now the aides tuned primarily to Indiana, sought ever smaller villages where hopefully they might avoid some of the shrieking teenagers who had so lovingly pursued Kennedy throughout the campaign and who showed up again and again on television. It was, they knew, counterproductive to their parents, and their parents could vote, and were not likely to vote for their daughter's singing idol or that ilk. Yet even in the little towns the campaign rhythm remained one of constant, concentric circles formed by age and passion. The inner circle was very very young, too young but passionate, "Who cares if his hair is a silly millimeter longer?" said the sign. The voters of 1972 and *1976*. The second ring was a mixed bag, still young, but of voting age; a few signs pro, a few signs against: "Defoliate Bobby," "Give Your Blood to American Troops Not the Vietcong." Then finally on the outer ring, quietly coming and listening and watching; neither jumping nor cheering nor stealing his cuff links, nor untying his tie, the good citizens of Indiana. They were often outside hearing range, for the sound equipment was uniformly terrible. There was no portable bull horn; it had been suggested but Ethel Kennedy had vetoed it. A bull horn, she said, looked too coarse on television, too much like Lyndon Johnson. They had come, the good Hoosiers, to see another one of those Kennedys.

They wondered if he were ready, and whether he was as good and as nice as Jack. "He isn't as handsome as Jack," said the woman in Peru, Indiana. "No," said the woman with her, "but he's still handsome just the same." They tried to measure him to sense whether or not he could be trusted. They would come and hear the shouting kids and wonder what it was all coming to anyway, and where it was all going to. The same question sometimes bothered the candidate.

There was already a ritual and an almost narcotic rhythm to the campaign, though it was still very early. The plane would land and, even if it was a smooth landing, everyone would clap; if it was rough, there would be enormous cheering. Everyone would then spill out of the plane. The aides would curse the local advanceman for not bunching up the crowd at the airport; instead it had been spilled all around the airport fence and would not show up on television ("always get a hall which is a little too small," said the same aide.) The band would play the Kennedy fight song, "This Man is Your Man," to the tune of "This Land is Your Land." Music by W. Guthrie; lyrics by T. Sorensen. There were the inevitable dogged McCarthy fans to heckle. One sensed that if Kennedy landed in a blizzard in Alaska at 3 A.M. in 1976 there would be five McCarthy people with homemade signs saying "Why Did You Wait Bobby?" or "McCarthy, Our Profile in Courage." "The McCarthy people always look like they're either going to or coming from a Quaker meeting," said a reporter.

Then a brief airport speech: I think we can do better in America, I think we can turn America around. Much cheering though the sound system does not work. Into bus and down into the heart of town; reporters screaming at bus driver not to lose contact with the lead car, not to let sightseers slip in the motorcade (A reminder of Dallas. For another Dallas was always in the back of everyone's mind and in Logansport, one day, Kennedy was speaking when we happened to look up to the roof of a building. There was a cop up there, poised with a telescopic rifle. It was a frightening sight. Someone asked the police chief what the cop was doing. "We want this man to leave our town the same way he entered it," he said.) Same speech in town, closing with the words (as Kennedy gave them) of George Bernard Shaw; "Some people see things as they are and ask why; I dream of things that never were and ask why not?" Shaw was basic to the campaign; he was the signal for reporters, making their phone calls or grabbing coffee, to run for the bus. Indeed, on occasion Kennedy closed a speech saying, "as George Bernard Shaw used to say, 'run for the bus.' "

We'd land in the next town and Dick Tuck, the wagonmaster, would look at the crowd and say that at least 50,000 people were waiting for us and had been waiting for six hours. Tuck looks, and there is no other word to describe him, bawdy. He is the surviving humorist of American politics; Tuck, the man who put the girl spy on the Goldwater train; who once hired a stewardess on Goldwater's plane to ask him whether he wanted coffee, tea or hemlock. He ran for state senator in California, making the Los Angeles river, which is dry, his major issue. "Either fill it up or paint it blue."

The great Tuck specialty, however, was the haunting of Richard Nixon. Tuck prepared a sign in Chinese for a Nixon visit to Chinatown which said, when translated in the newspapers the next day, "What About the Hughes Tool Loan?" Tuck hired a sweet little old lady to greet Nixon after the first Kennedy-Nixon television debate: "Don't worry, son. Kennedy beat you last night, but I'm sure you'll do better next time." (Later in 1968 Tuck worked at the

Republican convention for Nelson Rockefeller, where, among other things, he hired a group of pregnant women to carry signs reading: "Nixon is the One.")

Now Tuck was vaguely in charge of the press. As we drove into town he'd note that the bus driver estimates the crowd at the airport between 7,800 and 78,000. Though it was a clear day he'd add that "this crowd is much larger than the crowd Richard Nixon drew ten days ago on a day when it was not raining nearly as hard as it is today." He'd also quote several unidentified local officials at the airport saying they have just switched over from McCarthy. "You didn't talk to them?" he'd ask, surprised. Earlier in the day a reporter had complained that the candidate deviated from the prepared text. "Robert Kennedy is not a text deviate," Tuck snapped.

These were tough, exhausting days, beginning early in the morning, fifteen, sixteen speeches, endless trips, bumps in the sky, private interviews in the back of the plane for those that demanded them. "Senator, there's a Danish reporter who's come all the way over to see your campaign." There was trouble with one Dutch reporter who turned out not to be a reporter but a Dutch politician come aboard to study American politics and the Kennedy style so that he might try the same thing out on the Dutch. Then there'd be strategy conferences between the air pockets, and at stop after stop the same speech: I'm not satisfied with America the way it is; I think that we can do better; I think the violence and the divisions are unacceptable, and so I ask for your hand. And the humor to blunt the ruthless image which pursued him relentlessly. I talked to my brother Edward (great laughs because of the family), and asked him for some campaign buttons, and they arrived, 15,000 of them (small laughs of anticipation), and they all had his picture on them (big laugh now), and I told him he couldn't do that, I was the candidate (small laugh), and it was too late to enter the race, and besides, people would say he was ruthless (big laugh).

The campaign began in Indiana, and it was the search for a domino. Most campaigns begin in New Hampshire, a land of journalist overkill, with television reporters outnumbering Hampshiremen. New Hampshire is usually bigger than life; candidates die there and are born there, and it would have been a nice piece of turf for Robert Kennedy. New England, friendly, compact; a state where they still had all the old voter cards, and no kickback against the blacks there, not with that fine Protestant ethic. Even the hard core of Johnson's strength against McCarthy, those blue-collar workers who had voted for the President, were largely Catholic and would have gone to Kennedy, a more ethnically Catholic candidate than McCarthy. But they had let New Hampshire slip away. They had entered too late and Indiana was the first available primary. They came charging in, hoping that somehow Indiana would come around and then topple Nebraska; and then they would topple Oregon which would topple California, which would topple Mayor Daley, the fifty-first state. So the Kennedys were running hard but a little late. Three days after the announcement they had flown to Alabama and Tennessee, taking a regular flight to Atlanta, and chartering small planes over to Tuscaloosa. The charter man in Atlanta wanted some kind of proof of credit, having apparently read somewhere that the rich are the slowest in the world to part with their money, and so Fred Dutton, Kennedy's traveling aide, whipped out his Carte Blanche card and $1,800 worth of charter was charged to it. This was all fine, except that the rich *are* slow paying, and by June an angry Carte Blanche was threatening to suspend credit to Attorney Dutton unless he quickly paid his bill. It was symbolic of the entire campaign. In 1960 the Kennedys had planned everything long in advance, the preliminary trips had started in 1957 and 1958, the early scouting; then the candidate showed himself visually to the delegates and Ted Sorensen, carrying a little notebook, checked out the delegates. By 1960, when Jack Kennedy announced, the basic organization and strategy was already laid out; responsibility already carefully delegated. Now in 1968 they were instinct-shooting. The events were running ahead of the men; until the very day that Robert Kennedy announced, most of them thought they would be sitting it out until 1972. He entered on March 16, and Teddy called Gerard Doherty, one of Teddy's men: Look Gerry, you take Indiana. On March 22, he arrived there, with a week to get 5,500 signatures for the filing. Everywhere panicked phone calls were going out, and people were told to get down to Indiana. Why? asked one woman, a dedicated political worker in 1960 but now a mother of two. Because we need you, they said. Need me to do what? she asked. We don't know yet. But get down here by Friday; and off she went. So if they were running a little late they were also running very hard, with almost desperate energy; a campaign pieced together at the last minute. Two students from Fordham were put in charge of forty from Ohio State because they arrived at volunteer headquarters four hours ahead of the larger group, and pulled their assignments first. They were all, in the flurry of activity, sent to a white working-class neighborhood where they were less than welcome. If these blue-collar whites wanted to hear about Robert Kennedy, they did not want to hear about him from some smart-aleck college kids who should have been off at college studying a little harder, and who had probably burned their draft cards anyway. Eventually the kids were moved to a black ward where they were warmly welcomed and made common cause. Much of it was like this, and in many ways the Kennedys were curiously unsure of themselves despite their reputation for slickness and for being a part of the well-oiled Kennedy machine. ("Does the powerful Kennedy machine have any more typewriter paper?" asked a secretary on the plane one day.) Indeed they were so unsure of themselves that they had carefully and gratefully listened to the advice of one Gordon St. Angelo, the Indiana state chairman. The nice Mr. St. Angelo had given them all kinds of friendly advice, such as, "Stay out of Indiana." They had liked him, had thought of him as Their Mr. St. Angelo, only to discover once in Indiana, having disregarded his advice, that he was no friend at all, that he wished dark days for them, and had indeed devoted most of his working hours to calling press conferences where he discussed how much the Kennedys were spending in Indiana, buying all those votes, a tactic which, he confided to a reporter, was by far the most effective way to attack the Kennedys. They did not like Mr. St. Angelo and somehow, later, one sensed Mr. St. Angelo would get his.

The staff was briefed everywhere on what was obvious about Indiana: a conservative state, strong Ku Klux Klan in the old days, more like Kentucky and Tennessee than anything else; go easy on the race. So they were running a somewhat muted campaign, fearing both fore-lash and backlash. The problem was part religious and part racial. Southern Indiana was part of a great religious belt which began in the Midwest, heading southwest through Tennessee and Kentucky into Oklahoma (Oklahoma, traditional Democratic territory, had given Richard Nixon one of the largest percentages of victory in 1960), and in some of these areas the more fundamentalist churches were militantly anti-Catholic: preacher after preacher had taken the pulpit to campaign if not for Richard Nixon then against Jack Kennedy. The issue had burned like a brush fire, costing Jack immense numbers of votes. He had eased the religious issue some; he was young and handsome and did not look like a Catholic, and television had helped to break down some of the older prejudices. But if prejudices die, they die slowly, particularly in an area undergoing some economic difficulty, and in 1968 some of it was still there. (Larry O'Brien, one of the architects of the 1960 strategy which had been so dependent upon winning every single primary, proving that a handsome young Catholic could win, could still offer small and fervent prayers to Stuart Symington who, for reasons known only to God, had chosen not to enter Indiana in 1960.) And there was prejudice against Negroes too, and Robert Kennedy entered Indiana in the minds of white Indianans as the man most identified with the upward and now unruly thrust of the Negro. He was *their* candidate; he would go into their areas and be mobbed, much more so than Gene McCarthy, whose voting record was basically similar on race, but who seemed curiously dispassionate about that most passionate question. One looked at McCarthy on television and did not think of Negroes. McCarthy, like Nixon, seemed safer.

Kennedy faced many problems in Indiana and he had barely been in the race a week when the entire campaign changed. One night, with a minimum of fanfare, Lyndon Johnson withdrew as a candidate for reelection. Historians and reporters will speculate for years as to why Johnson did it, what his motives were. The most likely explanation is that he found himself tied to a hopelessly unpopular war and likely to be ravaged in the primaries by two critics and beaten by Kennedy, the politician he hated the most. As such he decided to withdraw as a candidate; and hope for one last chance to find peace. That destroyed Kennedy's most important issue, the war, and more important, removed his favorite opponent, for it was Johnson who made him look good, made him a necessity. Many liberals, uneasy about Kennedy, could now, with Johnson departed, relax and smile at McCarthy again. Gene McCarthy, who often seemed to be a more incisive analyst than candidate, had said with considerable prophecy the day Johnson withdrew that it would hurt Bobby the most because until then Bobby had played the role of Jack Kennedy campaigning against Lyndon Johnson. Now it was going to be much more difficult, it was going to have to be Robert Kennedy campaigning against Jack. Kennedy's opponents in Indiana were clean Gene McCarthy, a tough-minded candidate of considerable subtlety who was running on a similar platform (How do you attack McCarthy when you want his army? If you offend him, you offend his army), and Roger Branigin, the pleasant folksy governor. But these men were not his real opponents, the real opponent was Robert Kennedy himself. Finally he was the issue, and he was campaigning against himself, against the old fears and the old suspicions, though they might be different in different parts of the country. In the spring of this crucial year he had managed, because of his delayed entrance, to be at once too ruthless and too gutless for the liberals and the students, too radical for the middle class, too much the party man for some of the intellectuals, and too little the party man for most of the machines. He had, then, the look of a man who intended to rock the boat, and rock it he probably would. He was in that mood, he sensed the country needed a little rocking.

The suspicions of the good Hoosiers did not surprise him. Indeed he had anticipated and welcomed them. He had assumed they would have doubts about him for he knew who he was, and what he had come to champion in America, and he knew something about them and thus he assumed their doubts (indeed at times he would campaign hard, perhaps a little too hard, to ease their fears and suspicions), but the liberal suspicions, and the depth and intensity of them, had hurt and surprised him. He knew his own mistakes and he was willing to live with them, but now the animosity of the liberals shocked him. The liberal suspicions were not exactly new; they came and bloomed seasonally about the Kennedys. They existed about John Kennedy on his way to the White House, for Adlai Stevenson was their candidate then, and faded when Kennedy attained it. Indeed by the time of his death they had almost forgotten about Stevenson—so much so when one of the high priestesses of New York liberalism was asked to contribute to the Adlai Stevenson Institute in Chicago, she said no darling, *live* politicians were her hobby. They existed about Robert Kennedy, especially because he looked and acted more Irish than his brother and had that McCarthy committee in his background. They faded upon his performance as Attorney General, bloomed again when he became an instant New Yorker on his way to the Senate, when he challenged Ken Keating, a man with a reasonably liberal record and who had identified himself regularly with Israel ("Keating," the sign said in 1964, "Nasser's Number One Enemy, Israel's Number One Friend"). The suspicions faded even more in the late sixties, upon his performance as a Senator, and with the real fear of the war and the backdrop of The Man. They who had once feared him, and even perhaps voted for Ken Keating, had spent October and November depressed about the prospect of the forthcoming Johnson-Nixon-

Wallace race. They had loved him in the fall; they thought
of him often and remembered what was good in his brother's
administration and in his own record. Jack Kennedy would
never have sent combat troops to Vietnam, they decided.
Kennedy had thought of them often in this crucial time;
he had played brinkmanship with the race, and had then
entered gracelessly, rudely, and it now had all come back.
But he was in, nonetheless, joining in this extraordinary
campaign which had seen one after another of the traditional maxims fall.

Kennedy's own presence had helped transform the
campaign; he had done what McCarthy might not have
been able to do alone: he had driven Lyndon Johnson out
and probably turned American policy on Vietnam around.
A grateful liberal community, freed from its fear of the
war and its fear of Lyndon Johnson, liberated momentarily
from the attacks of the New Left, was celebrating its new
freedom amid its old suspicions and dislikes of Robert
Kennedy. It was symbolic of the fresh breezes suddenly
flowing in American politics in the spring that the liberals
once more had the luxury of disliking Robert Kennedy. He
had helped slay the dragon only to become the dragon.

It was the race issue, not Vietnam, which hung over the
campaign in Indiana. This was due in part to Johnson's
withdrawal and the Paris peace talks which had so suddenly
begun; with that Vietnam ebbed as an issue. (Abner Mikva,
an attractive reform candidate in a liberal Chicago district,
had said that up until March 31, you could not say hello to
anyone in his district without their saying, "Hello-how-are-
you-where-do-you-stand-on-Vietnam." "But after March 31,
people looked away whenever you mentioned Vietnam; they
did not want to hear about it, wanted to believe it had

gone away. They only wanted to hear what you were going to do about *them,* and all this rioting.") For this was a far different time from 1960 when John Kennedy could easily put together the blacks and the blue-collar whites. Now both the whites and the blacks were restless, and it was indicative of the situation that in Gary, one of Indiana's few big industrial cities, a mayoralty primary had broken down almost fifty-fifty between the black wards and the blue-collar white wards; Robert Kennedy had been with the blacks on that one. In 1968 one sensed everywhere the new movement toward racial polarization, an ever spiraling hostility and a breakdown in communications. The racial gap seemed wider than ever, and seemed to be getting yet wider. The gap was not being narrowed, as good liberal Americans had assumed, and as it had for the Jews and the Italians and everyone before. The rich were getting richer in America, and the poor were getting poorer, and by and large the rich were white and the black were poor. The public schools which had allowed previous classes of American underprivileged to break out of their ghettos were now simply one more enforcer of the existing conditions. Schools confirmed existing inequities, graduating functional illiterates, showing the brighter black kids that it was really hopeless.

They seemed angrier daily, as the promise of America failed to come through for them, and sensed acutely their own poverty in an affluent nation. Their moderate leaders were now being seriously undermined. They had told their people to keep working, keep praying, and somehow it all would be arranged; the heart of America was good and Christian. But there had been too few victories. The awakening which had begun with the outlawing of school segregation in 1954 and had continued with the various street protests was now out of control; the taste glands had been whetted, awakened and accelerated. More radical leaders were springing up, thanks to television. As in white politics, television was diminishing the old established order. Formerly the Negro leadership had been tightly structured and perhaps a little compromised because their organizations were somewhat dependent on white support, but now radical leaders were springing up without traditional structured organizations. With the aid of television, they were now being catapulted headlong into living rooms, those of black and white alike, on the basis of their looks, their anger, their ability to speak. There was a heightening of consciousness, and a sharpening of the sense of anger, for now the expectations were far ahead of the white society's ability to deliver.

Worse, the white society, so deeply involved in the war in Vietnam, seemed not to realize that it was failing to deliver. The young were threatened by the draft, were forced to go to hopeless schools which would prepare them for guaranteed third-class jobs. Watching their televisions, they saw the anger in other cities. The mood became increasingly angry and violent. Those who had been the followers of non-violence in the early sixties had turned off; they let their hair grow out into the new Afro style; racial pride was now emphasized; Malcolm X, who had been largely a joke to much of black America in 1960, seemed the prophet now with his black pride and black consciousness and his view that the core of the problem was not black inferiority but white immorality. (Feiffer caught some of the mood in a cartoon strip which showed an angry young black with a beard and dark glasses, saying: "As a matter of racial pride we want to be called 'blacks' . . . which has replaced the term 'Afro-American' . . . which replaced 'Negroes' . . . which replaced 'colored people' . . . which replaced 'darkies' . . . which replaced 'blacks.' ")

The nation seemed headed toward a kind of modified economic apartheid. It was moving very quickly toward it: whites leaving the cities for the suburbs, taking the good jobs and the favorable tax structure from the cities; white collars around poor, rotting black cores; the Negroes frustrated, living in slum conditions and unable to find decent jobs. If they found decent jobs, then they were unable to find decent housing and decent schools. Now the young blacks were totally outside the system, it meant nothing to them, held no promise. They would as soon destroy it as try and grope their way up it, and so they began to riot, tearing and burning down their black slums, their faces contorted with rage. It was the rage, not the causes of it, which showed up on white television sets; the whites, seeing that anger and that hatred, were now more frightened than ever. They decided, well, the hell with them, if that's the way they want to be, after all we've done for them; I always thought they were like that, and now the politicians are giving in to them too easily. Thus more whites moved to the suburbs, leaving behind only the blacks and those very poor whites who hated the blacks the most. So in early 1968 America was facing a social crisis of spectacular proportions, and it was ill-prepared. The country was hardly united. The last time there was a comparable crisis was the Great Depression, but then everyone was poor. The Congress of the United States and the president of the United States represented the poor. Now the poor were largely invisible; they had precious little representation; and they were on the outside of a society which was affluent, a society which looked around and saw the visible Negro, the middle-class Negro who had benefited from the progress of the last fourteen years, who was now super-visible. White America felt, Let the rest of them be like that; after all, we worked our way up (when a young Irish nun who worked in Chicago's west side, which is a jungle not even a ghetto, pleaded with Mayor Daley to come out there to *see* the conditions, the Mayor said, "Look, Sister, you and I came from the same place. We knew how tough it was. But we lifted ourselves up by the bootstraps..."). It was increasingly prepared to answer the Negro's anger by building bigger walls around the ghetto and sending more police in. Lyndon Johnson was imprisoned by the war in Vietnam and the complexities of the ghettos seemed far beyond his comprehension. Perhaps it was a generational thing, but he was still talking about the civil rights bills he had passed. Besides, those people who were protesting the ghettos most vigorously were also those who were protesting the war in Vietnam most vigorously, and that did not help their cause very much. So the polarization intensified.

But the polarization posed serious problems for any serious politician, white or black. It was difficult to talk to both societies at once, the poor angry black America and the affluent smug white one, which wanted black progress on *its* terms. If Martin Luther King, a moderate in 1964, talked as a moderate in 1967–68, he would lose his black constituency because he would seem too conservative, too much a Tom; yet if he talked radical, which would retain his black constituency and which he was now doing, he was in danger of losing the white semi-establishment following which was so basic to his cause. Similarly, if Robert Kennedy made the extra effort, as he did for three years, to walk in the ghettos, and talk to the leaders and represent their views on a national scale, then he immediately endangered himself among the whites as looking too radical, too identified with the blacks; perhaps he was even causing some of that restlessness, encouraging them to riot. It was becoming increasingly difficult in America, in 1968, to have any meaning in the black community and any credibility in the white. It was a simple fact of political life that there was a certain amount of happenstance in Kennedy's attempt to do it; anyone else as identified with blacks (and the view of Ken-

nedy was that you had to make that identification, the
country desperately needed someone who had some meaning for the Negro populace, otherwise they would turn off
the country completely) would nominally have lost the
whites. But he as a Kennedy, with that residue of glamour,
and also as a Catholic (who moved the Slavs and the blue-
collar working class), might be able to do it. Lindsay, as
strong with the blacks, had a good deal more trouble with
the blue-collar voters. So now, in 1968, Robert Kennedy was
trying to put all the odd pieces back together. He was trying
to keep the Negroes, who loved him with an intensity that
was special in such a rich country, to bring back the kids
and the liberals, and to hold on to the blue-collar whites as
well. Perhaps a Kennedy could do what no one else in
America could do, could walk that particular narrow path.
He was doing reasonably well in the early days of April,
talking about the divisions in the country; the need to be
generous; saying we must end this divisiveness, we must
work together; these problems can be handled, America
has the capacity and the generosity to deal with them. On
April 4, he went before a huge audience at Ball State University in Muncie, Indiana, and he spoke of this hope for
a generous America, and during the question and answer
period a young Negro asked him:

"You are placing great faith in white America. Is this
faith justified?"

Kennedy answered, simply. Yes. And then added: "I
think the vast majority of white people want to do the decent
thing." And that was what he believed. He felt that most
white people simply did not know what it was like to be
a black man in their own country, what the schools and
the housing were like; they did not understand the historical
conditions which had created the black man's dilemma.

Then he boarded his plane to fly to Indianapolis and, as he did, an aide told him that Martin Luther King had been shot, was seriously wounded, and was probably dying in Memphis. He seemed staggered and for a while he did not mention Dr. King. When he finally began to talk he said, "To think that I just finished saying that white America wants to do the right thing, and even while I was talking this happened." It gets worse and worse, he said, "all this divisiveness, all this hate. We have to do something about the divisions and the hate."

He landed in Indianapolis and learned that yes, it was true, and Dr. King was dead. Then he went on to a previously scheduled rally in the ghetto area; he had not wanted to go, but others convinced him he must honor this obligation. He spoke to an audience which was primarily black and he told them the news about Dr. King. In the background you could hear the gasps and the wails, and then he gave, extemporaneously, perhaps the best speech of the campaign, perhaps the best speech of his life:

> Martin Luther King dedicated his life to love and to justice for his fellow human beings, and he died because of that effort. In this difficult day, in this difficult time for the United States, it is perhaps well to ask what kind of a nation we are and what direction we want to move in. For those of you who are black—considering the evidence there evidently is that they were white people who were responsible—you can be filled with bitterness, with hatred and a desire for revenge. We can move in that direction as a country in great polarization—black people among black, white people among white, filled with hatred toward one another.
>
> Or we can make an effort, as Martin Luther King did, to understand and to comprehend and to replace that

violence, that strain of bloodshed that has spread across our land, with an effort to understand and love.

For those of you who are black and are tempted to be filled with hatred and distrust, at the injustice of such an act, against all white people, I can only say I feel in my heart the same kind of feeling. I had a member of my family killed, but he was killed by a white man. But we have to make an effort in the United States, we have to make an effort to understand, to go beyond these rather difficult times. My favorite poet was Aeschylus. He wrote: "Even in our sleep, pain which cannot forget falls drop by drop upon the heart until in our own despair against our will, comes wisdom through the awful grace of God."

What we need in the United States is not division, what we need in the United States is not hatred, what we need in the United States is not violence or lawlessness, but love and wisdom and compassion toward one another, and a feeling of justice toward those who still suffer within our country, whether they be white or whether they be black. So I shall ask you tonight to return home to say a prayer for the family of Martin Luther King, that's true, but more important to say a prayer for our own country, which all of us love—a prayer for understanding and that compassion of which I spoke. We can do well in this country, we will have difficult times, we've had difficult times in the past. We will have difficult times in the future. It is not the end of violence. It is not the end of lawlessness. It is not the end of disorder. But the vast majority of white people and the vast majority of black people in this country want to live together, want to improve the quality of our life, and want justice for all human beings who abide in our land. Let us dedicate ourselves to what the Greeks wrote so many years ago: to tame the savageness of man and make gentle the life of this world. Let us dedicate ourselves to that, and say a prayer for our country and for our people.

It was a sign of the changing new and angry times that Kennedy's very appearance in the ghetto was considered more important by the press than his speech. He was one of the rare American political figures who could, on a night of such anger and vengeance, go safely into the black quarters of the cities; others would go that night, and in the nights to follow, in unmarked cars or fly quickly over in helicopters as city after city burned.

They had been tied together, King and Kennedy, in what was essentially the same cause: working within the system to bring white and black together. They had both worked, for the last eight years, to make America more tolerable for the black. It was Robert Kennedy's phone call to a Georgia judge which had sprung King from jail in 1960, and which had probably won Jack Kennedy not only the election, but the affection of King's father, Martin King Sr.—a hard Baptist preacher with no love for white men and particularly for Catholics. (He later told reporters that he had planned to vote for Nixon because he did not trust Catholics, but would now vote enthusiastically for Kennedy. "Imagine Martin Luther King having a father who's a bigot," Jack Kennedy said later. "Well, we all have our fathers. . . .") The relationship after John Kennedy's election had been guarded, King and the Kennedys were not of the same style, and they were mutually suspicious at first. King felt that the Kennedys were dragging their feet on civil rights, which was correct—they simply did not understand how far there was to go and how slowly they were moving; and the Kennedys found King's brand of moralism somewhat heavy in the fast pragmatic world in which they operated, where idealism was carefully masked with cynicism. Nonetheless the justice department under Robert Kennedy was drawn increasingly into civil rights, not particularly because it wanted to be, but because the action was there and because the Kennedy administration, drawn in by events, had to come down on one side or the other, and finally there was only one side. By the end of the administration, the justice department virtually served as a coordinator for The Movement. It quietly lent its organizational skills to King and his people; organization had never been their strong point. They would choose an idea, more likely a target, jump in, and await the Lord to hand down the organizational plan, said one admiring follower. At the time of Jack Kennedy's assassination, Martin Luther King was holding higher hopes for Lyndon Johnson than he did for the late President (though Robert Kennedy was another matter, King had high hopes for him). He had seen in Johnson a son of the South trying to cleanse his past, had thought him deeply committed on civil rights, and anxious to prove his liberation. (This might have been a double miscalculation on King's part; he was from the South and Johnson was from the South, and perhaps both of them had thought the battle front would remain in the South. It was an area and a set of problems which Johnson understood far better than the problems of the ghettos.) Then the war came along, dominating the Johnson years and destroying the Great Society. Those years particularly undermined moderate leaders like King, who preached non-violence, love and reconciliation, hoping that the moral conscience of America would turn. It was a plea which did not particularly offend white America, but in the late sixties it fell on deaf ears among the alienated young blacks of the North. These young men were in the North because they had forsaken their past; the Protestant religion of their parents had failed, their god was dead; King was hot and they were cool. In the past year King had been pushed by events into increasing radicalism. His doubts about American society mounting, his criticism of the society sharpening, his white following diminishing, he was no longer so beloved by the white establishment. At the time of his death he had been organizing the Poor People's March on Washington. Had that failed, it was feared that it would have been one failure too many, and that the more radical leaders would take over his following, particularly among younger blacks. But now he was dead, the victim of one more assassin, and the campaign was breaking off. The Kennedys sent a plane to Memphis to bring King's body back to Atlanta, and all the great figures of America went to Atlanta.

In Atlanta there were additional dilemmas. The rioting had started throughout the country, and Chicago and Washington and Pittsburgh were burning. Lindsay's walk had helped ease tension in New York but the nation seemed to be just short of revolt. Kennedy wanted to go on national television and discuss what was happening, and why the Negroes were rioting, and there was discussion among a very few friends as to whether he should. His point was strong: most of white America would see only the rioting and the anger; Kennedy knew why this rioting was taking place and he thought people would listen to him, and besides, he felt the country needed some leadership at that moment. But he was warned that anything he might do would be misinterpreted, would be attributed to political motive. The rednecks would say, look at that damn nigger-lover, and the liberals would say, he'll exploit anything. Reluctantly he decided against it. Later that night an informal meeting between Kennedy and a number of black leaders took place. Though some of the men, such as the Reverend Ralph Abernathy and John Lewis, the former head of Snick, were sympathetic, almost all the black anger in America seemed to be unleashed on Kennedy in that room, one constant outpouring of bitterness. Why should we support a white man? Why should we bother with America's election? You people kill our leaders. Kennedy painfully tried to talk with them, not to answer them, saying "If you think I'm going to give you a campaign speech, you're mistaken. I'm not here to campaign. I'm sorry. I'm here to pay my respects to a friend and a leader. I can't campaign. I know how you feel and I know your anger, but I can't make a speech to you, I'm sorry."

The King funeral: a dark, somber affair, a broiling hot sun. Every important black man in the country was there. White leaders were everywhere. The little church was so crowded that the group of Senators which had flown down had to stay outside. There was only room for presidential candidates inside. King's people were wearing their poor people's uniforms as badges of honor. One of King's people was trying to move the enormous crowd in front of the church so that the mule-drawn wagon would be able to start. The crowd refused to move. He was begging them now, "Make it easier for the family, this is a way to honor Martin," but they refused to move. They have moved too often at the requests of officials all their lives, and they will not be moved. Then the march from the church to Morehouse College. More than five miles under the grueling sun. It was a strange assemblage of the mighty and the poor. It went through Atlanta; stores all closed, in honor of Dr. King, and in honor of keeping them from being destroyed (Rich's, the famous store, closed its downtown store, but left its suburban store open. Perhaps there is no honor in the suburbs). Along the way some of the older Negroes began to lead in singing; the walk had become a shuffle, slow, hot, burdened. Someone tried "We Shall Overcome," but it seemed tainted. Rather, they moved back to some of the older ones.

> *I'm on my way to Freedom*
> *We shall Not be Moved*
> *I'm on my way to Freedom*

We shall not be moved
Just like a tree that's planted near the water
We shall not be moved.

Martin's gone ahead
But we shall not be moved
Martin's gone ahead
But we shall not be moved
Just like a tree that's planted near the water
We shall not be moved.

"I'm coming Martin," someone wailed, "I'm coming now," and the rest said, yes, yes, we're coming.

Along the route Kennedy became the star. As we got closer to Morehouse there were crowds of Negroes standing in front of their houses, handing out cool water to marchers. When Kennedy came along, slight, almost hard to find in the crowd, they began to clap, *Yes, Bobby, Bobby,* and more clapping. "It's as if they're anointing him," a friend of mine said. Someone else complained later that even here he was campaigning. Perhaps, but it seems American, in 1968, that a funeral should be part of the campaign.

Several days later we were talking during a break in the campaign; Kennedy started discussing the fabric of America. I said that it seemed very thin, stretched far too thin; there has been so much violence that any quality of doubt or buffer has been used up, now everyone believes the worst. There were 50,000 people or more at the funeral, many of them the best people in the country, all having come to make a witness, all this passion, and yet, all it would have taken was one nut, pulling one trigger or throwing one bomb, to have set off the entire country. Yes, said Kennedy with a touch of bitterness, the richest country in the world. White people living better than they ever did before; no matter who they are, having it better: if they had rented, now they own. If they had ridden buses or walked, now they own one or two cars. If they had sweated, now they have a summer place. Now they go out to dinner once or twice a week. But all they think about is how much they have to pay in taxes, and how much more they pay in taxes than five or ten years ago. It is extraordinary how ungenerous they have become, he said. They don't see the poor and they don't want to.

All this distrust, he said, everyone in America distrusting everyone else. Then he became very critical of President Johnson: he never went into a ghetto. He knew he had the Negroes and decided they had nowhere else to go, and he didn't care about the ghettos. He was going to run on crime in the streets, and they knew this, knew that he felt he didn't have to go after their votes. Look at Dr. King, he couldn't get through to the White House, the administration wouldn't see him. They thought he was an enemy because of Vietnam. So the Negroes felt more and more isolated politically.

I nodded, yes, but how much of it could really be blamed on the President? Wasn't it a little too easy to blame it all on Johnson? How much of it was the diverse pull of the country; perhaps we had become too rich, and as such, less dependent on each other, allowing the selfish rather than the dependent tendencies to become dominant. So that now the things which divided us were stronger than the things which united us. We were not bound together tightly, but were permitted the luxury of divergent pulls. People behaved best in adversity, worst in luxury. His face darkened for a minute; after all, what I was saying was that if he became president he would end up as beaten by the system as Johnson had been. Then, rather coldly, the informality of the last ten minutes gone, he said, "I don't think so at all. I think the country wants to be led and needs to be led. I think it wants to do the right thing." And then he was off campaigning and moving again.

From the funeral he flew back to Indiana, ending up in Terre Haute in Southern Indiana. It has the look of a depressed city. (One develops a fine eye for poverty in America after campaigning. One can sense where the money has departed and where the money and the jobs have arrived.) In the downtown area, store fronts were closed. Terre Haute was cool to the candidate. It was the day after the King funeral, and white America, by and large, was not mourning Dr. King, rather it was frightened by the violence which took place in the wake of the assassination, and it felt that the politicians were too permissive. As he rode into town several people shouted coon-catcher, coon-catcher, at him. His speech was weak and edgy and somewhat defensive on civil rights; with a new emphasis on the fact that the violence is unacceptable. The audience was almost entirely white, only a couple of Negroes there. I asked one what he thought was happening. "Oh he's my man. He's my man all right." What about the rest of Terre Haute? "These people? These people?" and he laughed. That night several of the reporters claimed that in the last day Kennedy had been trimming on civil rights. His staff denied it, but the reporters insisted. The talk was pleasantly abrasive, and everyone was in a reasonably good mood because the schedule had eased off a bit, for a day, and there was time to eat for a change. One of the reporters kept telling one of the young speech writers, "What I can't stand about your guy, what I find hard to stomach, is that back right after the war, when I came home, and I led an open housing drive on the campus, and it was a lonely fight, your guy was on the McCarthy committee. That's what I can't stand. And now he's a big liberal." One of the speech writers, who was approximately eight years old when this transpired, was enjoying it all, saying, "You should have had a richer father that's all. That was your first mistake." It was all reasonably good natured, but it could have gone sour at any minute. The staff was restless; there was too much time and they were not used to it. We had checked into the hotel in the early afternoon and there was nothing scheduled until the next morning. "Four colleges in the area and all of them on vacation when we got here. Best scheduling of the trip."

The next morning Kennedy breakfasted with a group of 150 women in Terre Haute and gave a pedestrian speech. He was not a particularly good speaker, and here he was ill at ease. But then in the question-and-answer period, and this is equally typical, he was very good. He fielded their questions and he had decided that while they were all good Democrats, they were *complacent,* and so he got carried away on the subject of the poor in America. "They are hidden in our society. No one sees them any more. They're invisible. A small minority in a rich country. Yet I am stunned by the lack of awareness of the rest of us toward them and their problems. We don't see them. We pay all these taxes and pass all these programs to help them, and yet the programs don't reach them and the taxes go for other things, and every year their lives are more helpless than ever and yet we wonder what's wrong with them, after all we did for them." It went on like that, very good stuff, not exactly what the good ladies of Terre Haute had set out to hear, but it was very effective. There were almost no reporters present.

We got off to Gary which is a very tough town, perhaps the most polarized city in America. On the plane Kennedy talked about his problem in the state. Since the King funeral he had had two days of cold receptions. "So far in Indiana they seem to want to see me as a member of the black race —I don't think I can win if that happens. If it keeps up I'm lost. That breakfast was very good and you could feel them coming around, but how many people in Indiana will get that much exposure, how many chances will you have to talk at that length?" He stopped for a moment. "These people never ask me, 'What are you going to do about the Negro problem, or what can we do for the Negro?' They always ask: 'What are you going to do about the violence.'" Then he continued with a private and highly informed analysis of varying Negro groups in the country. He saw the Southern Christian Leadership Conference splitting apart inevitably with Dr. King dead. There are too many conflicting ambitions and conflicting pulls which have been kept submerged only because of the sheer power and prestige of King himself. Now with him gone, they will begin to surface. Besides, there is no one person who has all the qualities of Dr. King: one is his intellectual equal, another has his ability to speak, another has his instinct for the moral position and how to dramatize it, but no one had all the pieces like Dr. King. What about Stokely and Rap? someone asked. Beyond bringing in, he said, it's all gone too far. They're too bitter, been hit on the head, harassed and arrested too many times. As far as America goes, you can forget about them; your only hope is the other young Negroes. Keep them in, and give them alternatives, and make it possible for them to stay inside the system. It can be done, but you have to move quickly and you have to be willing to take some heat in the process. I mean, they're not going to tell you how grateful they are.

Kennedy had been making a major part of his pitch on the ghettos an attempt to get private industry involved. He had decided that there had been too much reliance in the past upon government action, and that nothing could be done in the ghettos until there were jobs available. This put him in a different group from most of the older Democrats who, from the New Deal days, had an instinctive reliance on the government's ability to handle any problem; but it did put him in the rough category of younger men, like Chuck Percy of Illinois, who felt that government's encouraging business to operate in the ghetto would have more long-term results than overdependence on government programs. It also put him at odds with some of his allies.

Michael Harrington, the young socialist who had articulated the plight of the poor in America, had switched from McCarthy to Kennedy despite the reliance on the private sector, and in Indiana Dick Goodwin brought Harrington in to meet the candidate. "I guess you don't like all the things I say about free enterprise," Kennedy said.

"I guess you don't like all the things I say about socialism," Harrington answered.

Goodwin interjected: "Mike told the television people he couldn't support Rockefeller because Rockefeller wouldn't really spend 150 billion dollars for the cities."

Kennedy looked at Harrington, "My God, you didn't say I would, did you?"

Gary. A very tough town; it is black and white and not together; it is steel mills. The kind of city America's poets once wrote so lyrically about, *Oh I hear the blast of your furnaces, Oh America, the flame of your furnaces, the might of your steely strength.* Well, that was a long time ago. Now Gary seems to reek of all of America's urban ills, its drabness, *Oh I taste the sweet pollution of your air, Oh America, I see the blast of your furnaces covering the linen on my wash line.* Gary is depressing, one sees it and senses the revolt against the industrial revolution which is going on in America. Yes, the city brought them all here, the Negroes and the poor whites and the Slavs, and offered them jobs. They won their great battles, got their unions, kept their jobs, made good wages and yet now the quality of life often seems terrible. The reception for the candidate was mixed—unadulterated enthusiasm from the blacks, more cautious from the whites, who were interested but worried (a few "Bobby Ain't Jack" bumper stickers).

Much of the black reception appeared to be for Dick Tuck; he is something of a hero in Gary. He was dispatched there last fall, by Kennedy, to keep the Democratic machine of John Krupa from stealing the election from Dick Hatcher, the black candidate. Tuck, who knew exactly how a machine operates, kept the Krupa machine from voting the dead and the imaginary (and also kept about 5,000 Negroes on the register). He had heard of a plot to have all the voting machines in the black wards break down at the height of the voting, and so he sent off to nearby Chicago for ten Negro pinball machine repairmen, whose credentials he faked, and whom he tutored on a model of the voting machine. At one point Tuck warned them sternly when they began experimenting on how to run the totals a little higher so they registered too quickly. On election day, sure enough, when the machines started breaking down, always in the black wards, Tuck's men fixed them in minutes instead of hours. Tuck also beat the machine on another ploy traditional with machines which want to discourage Negro voting. The machine had been sending out registered letters to Negroes which said that there was some evidence that the individual was not properly registered. Naturally a registered letter terrifies people in ghettos since it usually means someone wants to reclaim something, wants money or plans an arrest. So the Negroes would not open the letters, and they would come back unopened and the machine could strike the blacks off the rolls. Tuck got hold of the lists and proved the letters were only going to blacks. When Hatcher was elected, Tuck became something of a folk hero in Gary, though he ran up a bill of $130 at Gary's Steel Club, which is where the local establishment meets and eats. As soon as the election was over he disappeared and there were great efforts to find him. The bill eventually ended up in Chicago with some Kennedy people there. After a few months, when Tuck arrived in town, someone presented him with the bill. He scanned it for a minute, and then said: "That's outrageous. I wouldn't pay it if I were you."

In Gary the whites remained edgy; there were few of them along the streets as the motorcade pulled through. Yet there were some around and some of them cheered, and considering the racial division in the city, even that was a hopeful sign. "They should really be hating him here," said one of his press people. "But maybe the magic still works." The audience in a Gary hall was about two to one black. The speech was good, mainly on the different vision of America that whites and Negroes have, and what America has promised and delivered or failed to deliver to each; how each sees a different thing. "Then the whites say, 'Why don't the Negroes come up and work hard and earn it like the Poles and the Italians?' But it's more difficult. The jobs have gone to the suburbs, or been taken over by machines, and are beyond the reach of them as they were not before with people of limited background."

But the Gary trip had gone reasonably well, and a week later, when the entourage made a trip on the famed Wabash Cannonball, the reporters, restless on the train ride, composed a song to the tune of "The Wabash Cannonball," called "The Ruthless Cannonball." One verse went:

He has the Poles in Gary
The blacks will fill his hall,
There are no ethnic problems
On the Ruthless Cannonball.

Then it was back to Indianapolis. The suspicion that
Kennedy had been trimming persisted. That night Mankiewicz was asked: "Will he place greater emphasis on reconciliation rather than divisiveness?"

It had been a long day for Mankiewicz and he answered, "Well, I think you can say he will not urge divisiveness."

One day out to go to West Virginia for a day of campaigning.
Why West Virginia? someone asked Tuck. "That's the only
way you can get news coverage," said Tuck. "You get it by
going in and out as many times as possible. Candidate
arrives, news, candidate leaves, news, candidate arrives
again. Television cameramen everywhere." The day in West
Virginia was a long nostalgic one: Robert retracing the
footsteps of his brother, telling the people how much the
Kennedy family owed to West Virginia. The crowds were
good in tiny town after tiny town. Kennedy talked about
economic progress, of bringing in industry, and yet it had
a hollow sound. One looked at the mountains, the gaps, and
the population, and one sensed the hopelessness of it, that
no new industry would come in here, and that the talented
young people would almost certainly have to leave. Some of
the stops were infinitesimally small. Oceana: so small that
no one seemed to want to give the population. Finally, it was
given as 3,000. Oceana is not even a crossroads, it is barely
a stop. The candidate stopped, and kids spilled all over
him and the car. "I want to be introduced in Oceana," he
said, "where's the Mayor?" Mayor. Where's the Mayor?

Someone was dispatched to find the Mayor. Eventually the Mayor, a balding man, materialized from the back of the crowd. "Mayor, say something nice about me. Introduce me." The Mayor looked at him; they had never met before. Then he got up on the car with Kennedy and said, "I give you the next President of the United States." It was the best and simplest introduction of the campaign. "Very good," says Kennedy, "We'll take you with us the rest of the way." A few words on America; that it must do better, and we departed from Oceana.

The day was long and hard and he ended it in Charlestown with what was billed as a major foreign-policy speech. This one was not about Vietnam, but rather about the Soviet Union and coexistence. It was absolutely appalling, perhaps the worst speech of the campaign. It read as though the first part of it was written in 1960, about showing the Russians our might, and the second part in 1968, about desperately searching for new ways of leaving the cold war behind. It seemed to alternate paragraphs in this manner, a truly bewildering piece of work. Kennedy himself seemed to understand the discrepancies, and became confused and embarrassed midway through. "You ought to introduce your speech writers to each other," one reporter later told him. Another added: "I thought you told those hawks where to get off." He paused. "Those doves, too." Kennedy laughed and took it well. He had been introduced that night by John D. (Jay) Rockefeller IV. Tall, thirty years old, a millionaire now serving in the West Virginia legislature and running, one knew, for Governor. And eventually, after that, for president (though perhaps he will be slowed down and have to run for vice-president first). The press knew all this and was annoyed. It was all too perfect; Rockefeller, tall, bespectacled, had sat up there with his wife, the former Sharon Percy of Illinois (he will cut into the Republican vote in Illinois), and what was worse and most galling, he had made a very intelligent and graceful introduction. Now in the back of the plane flying to Washington, Kennedy was praising him: hadn't young Jay Rockefeller given a fine speech, wasn't that good? The reporters were noticeably cool. They were annoyed by this instant celebrity and the fact that young Jay, unlike Uncle Nelson, had the good sense and the good fortune to join a party which might love him. One of them made a strongly anti-Young-Jay remark. You didn't like the speech, asked Kennedy, surprised. No, said the reporter, it isn't just the speech, it's the whole damn thing of him coming down here and practically buying a base, with all his money, and cashing in on his name. No, said Kennedy, he's better than that. He went to Japan and learned Japanese and did some good things there, and then he came back and he wanted to work in the poverty program and so he came down here, and he was very good at it. The people like him very much. Sure, sure, said one of the reporters, and what he was really saying was Must American politics be like this? Are we going to have only Kennedys and Rockefellers the rest of our lives? The atmosphere was getting a little tense. You guys are pretty rough, said Kennedy, what's your real objection? He's too ruthless, said a reporter, and everyone relaxed. Why did we spend the day in West Virginia? someone asked him. I don't know, he answered.

The campaign rested for one day in Washington; husbands met wives, children were reintroduced to fathers, there was a desperate search for clean socks, and then back to the plane early Monday morning. The plane was headed back to Indiana. On board, the candidate was in a good mood. "Are you ready for my speech?" he asked a reporter.

The reporter replied that he had memorized the Kennedy speech, had indeed amused many friends by giving it at cocktail parties on Sunday. "No, not *that* speech, my new speech about the four vice-presidents who came from Indiana. It's my best historical speech." I'm getting off the plane, the reporter replied. "Or my new speech on the Negroes," he said, mocking himself, mocking the clichés of American race, "how they're going too fast . . . how you can't expect people who have lived one way for more than 200 years to have everything overnight . . . and then my conclusion, that they have to earn their rights just like all the Americans did, all the other people who came to this country and worked hard and earned a place. Now it's their turn to make it on their own. . . ."

The plane started in the East, and it was filled with television teams, some working for the networks, some independent, some doing instant documentaries, some working for the candidate. Everywhere he went they followed. The candidate would come aboard, would stop to talk for a moment—How are you? How is your wife?—and all of television would move in, as if to inhale him. Your comments—wife has a headache—are recorded for posterity; every little word is gobbled up. It is the age of documented irrelevance. This sort of thing caused some anger among the working reporters, or writing press as they are affectionately known, the new minority in American journalism. ("Who's the pool TV man getting him when he shaves tomorrow?" asked one reporter.) The plane zipped across the sky, pushing through occasional turbulence. (Once when John Glenn, the astronaut, was traveling with him and the air was particularly bumpy, Kennedy turned to two reporters sitting behind him and said, "I have a small announcement to make: John Glenn is terrified.") Bloody Marys were broken out by the time the plane crossed the Appalachians; the drinks were there, they were free and there seemed to be no earthly reason not to drink them.

A campaign humor also began to emerge. Now when the reporters went to a restaurant and the food was late, they would say, the service is *unacceptable*, I think we can do better. Or on the genuinely terrible hotel rooms in Indianapolis: I think we can do better, I think we can turn the Indiana hotel industry around. Much of it, of course, fastened on Indiana. We had all been here too long; there was a constant laundry problem, and a constant food problem. Indiana, someone said, is where they say French dressing on your salad, and it's *orange*.

We landed in Indiana and everyone was relaxed. Mankiewicz was on the press bus and was now in particularly good form. We were off to Vincennes and other historical sights. "Vincennes, as you all know, was founded by George Rogers Clark. As you are all aware, Mr. Clark was credited with saying, 'don't trust anyone over thirty.' Now does anyone want to hear about William Henry Harrison?" Tell us about the pacification program, Frank, someone asked. "Well the pacification program is going reasonably well in Indiana," said Mankiewicz, picking up the Saigon language, "but you must remember that they are a proud people with a culture and a tradition all their own, and therefore these things take time. You can't expect things overnight. We Americans are too impatient, we expect too much." Someone asked how long Kennedy would stop in town. "I don't know," Mankiewicz answered. "First he'll make a speech. Then he'll answer some questions. Then he'll be besieged by a surging throng of mature adult voters."

Much of the humor was unfair, but Indiana was a state which had not changed, and much of it was rural and some of the reporters were bitter about being on an expense account in an area where there was so little opportunity to exploit it. But one did feel, in Indiana, that one had stepped back a bit in time. Later after the campaign, when Gene McCarthy was complaining about his defeat there, he would say of Indiana: "They kept talking about the poet out there. I asked if they were talking about Shakespeare, or even my friend Robert Lowell. But it was James Whitcomb Riley. You could hardly expect to win under those conditions."

This day had been given over to television. Kennedy was to campaign on several levels: the normal one which was to make an impact on the towns he visited, the secondary one which was to make an impact on the normal local, state and national coverage, and now a third one which was to create images which his own television teams could use for his television commercials. This last was perhaps the most vital part of the campaign; perhaps one percent of the voters might see him in the flesh, but through television almost all the voters would see him. So the day was devoted to television clips: Was he an outsider as Roger Branigin charged? A tourist? Part of the day was scheduled so that Robert Kennedy would visit and be filmed at every shrine in Indiana. He would come on the screen knowing Indiana's history and being reflected in it—the Lewis and Clark Memorial, the Lincoln Shrine. In addition, a major effort would be made to counter the ruthless image. Was he ruthless? The television clips would show him a little shy, wittier than people thought, a little slight, and he would not look ruthless but rather would look victimized by all that ruthless talk. Most important it would show him answering questions from the good people of Indiana. They would stumble a little in their questions, which would show the natural touch, though they wouldn't stumble too much. It would have a sense of real questions put by real people; the questioners must not look like they just came from doing a soap commercial, though they should not be too ugly either. Long leathered faces of farmers were very good because everybody trusts long leather-faced farmers. Everybody knows that they speak with eternal wisdom and that they are bothered by questions which bother everyone. As for students, they should not be too bearded. It would be better to have fairly clean-cut students.

Kennedy's advisers had learned long ago that he was far better at questions and answers, particularly tough questions, than he was at set speeches. At set speeches he tensed and went flat. In questions and answers he came alive; he felt challenged and felt a personal relationship with the questioner. In 1964, during his Senate race, the best television clips had come from a meeting with Columbia students; semi-hostile, they had poured it to him, tough ungenerous questions. The best part of him had responded; the intelligence, the candor and the humor had flashed through. Probably it had hurt Keating, for Keating had matched it with little of his own. The television clips for Kennedy had to be a little different than those for most candidates. For most candidates the job was simply to introduce him—here, this is what he looks like, and please get the good side of his face. With Kennedy it was different. Everyone knew what he looked like; along with Lyndon Johnson he was probably the best known public figure in America. The problem with Kennedy was the reaction to him. A lot of people recognized him and did not like what they recognized. When he was running for the Senate, he and his aides had discovered what they had already suspected—that he had a very high antipathy quotient, a polling measure developed by the firm of Bennett and Chaikin.

This test reflected the number of people who, when polled, registered a serious objection to a political figure. In 1964 Keating had what was to them an alarmingly low antipathy quotient of six. It surpassed even that of Dwight Eisenhower in 1956, which was seven. In 1964 when Lyndon Johnson's A.Q. was 17 (before the escalation), Robert Kennedy had a staggering A.Q. of 36, though many of the people who disliked him might vote for him. Now in Indiana the Kennedy people realized that they had a similar problem on their hands; and that while McCarthy might not be that well known, there were few people who felt strongly against him. All that particular day the advisers tried to get the candidate away from the crowds (which would reinforce the A.Q., showing the sweaty, unruly side of the candidate, or at least an image which projected as sweaty and unruly), and away from reporters. They tried to get him in an indigenous setting, with no teeny-boppers, this man is not discordant. They got him to tiny little crossroad stops, barred reporters, got him into general stores, and encouraged the people to ask questions: the quiet Kennedy in a quiet surrounding.

In addition, he did the usual twelve stops, his voice ragged at the end. The reporters were still claiming that he was cutting back on civil rights, which he was. (Someone had mentioned to Tuck that Kennedy was giving an Indiana speech, and Tuck became angry. "There is no Indiana speech. When are you guys going to learn that? The Indiana speech died in 1956. Anything you say here goes everywhere. These people here have seen the war just like everyone else, just like Chicago and New York. It's not 1930. If you ask the people in Indiana what concerns them it's not Indiana. The Governor is running around saying that the only issue is Indiana for Indianans and we're going to beat him on that; he's underestimating these people. There is no Indiana speech or a New York or Wisconsin speech. Learn that will you.") Late that night, after 11 P.M., Kennedy went to dinner with a few friends and magazine writers. It was very late and he was very tired; all the ideas about preserving the candidate, the conservation of the candidate's energy, were shot. There was just too much to do, and too little time, and besides, one of the problems of his campaign was that the candidate lacked a Robert Kennedy—someone who would do for him what he did for Jack Kennedy in 1960, who would handle all the endless details quickly and correctly and intelligently, and make sure the candidate himself was bothered with only a minimal amount of detail. That was hopeless now. These days he would campaign all day long and then go out very late at night to discuss the next day with aides—sometimes finishing dinner at 2 A.M.; drawing on his exceptional physical condition and energy. "You guys are always complaining about the fact that he doesn't go into detail on Vietnam and on civil rights in his short speeches," Dutton once said, "one reason is sheer fatigue. How much energy does a candidate have. Fourteen speeches a day and you want him to touch all the points on civil rights." That night he was talking about his main campaign poster. He did not like the photograph which was both boyish and surly boyish—"like the guitar player in a high school rock-and-roll band," he said.

"Like a bad guitar player in a bad high school band," Warren Rogers of *Look* corrected. Kennedy agreed.

The food was late, and he and John Glenn were both frequently interrupted by autograph hunters. Finally he turned to a friend and asked whether it was worth it, couldn't it just be done on television, couldn't you sit back and do it from the studios as some of his younger assistants were insisting. (Again the new politics/old politics split; the younger people thought most of the traditional campaigning was a waste of time and money, television could do it all. They wanted him to do less street campaigning, to pay less attention to newspapers.)

No, said Dick Goodwin, "You have to go out there and do it all and you have to show that you don't have contempt for them, that you value who they are."

"You could afford to do more by television if you weren't so rich," someone else said. "You're too rich not to get out there and mix. McCarthy ought to run a television campaign."

Someone else said that it was all insane, that it didn't matter any more. Visiting people was a thing of the past (though election results would consistently show that Kennedy ran better where he campaigned personally). The newspapers were a thing of the past. You didn't get any space from Pulliam (Eugene Pulliam was the arch-conservative owner of the two Indianapolis newspapers whose treatment of Kennedy and his campaign was scandalous). Forget it—it probably makes you a little bit of an underdog. Papers have less influence than anything else in this campaign.

But this too was quickly challenged. Newspapers, another aide said, were still important, in a limited sense. Not so much the reporters, except inasmuch as they can influence the columnists, and the columnists in turn influence other reporters, and finally the columnists influence the television commentators who still lack confidence of their own judgments. So one columnist saying one thing can trigger an entire series of comments. (Eugene McCarthy, referring to the same characteristic and a little bit bitter over his coverage and bitter about the American press in general, once compared all reporters to blackbirds sitting on a telephone wire. One flies off and they all fly off. One flies back and they all fly back.) Thus James Reston was very important and a campaign should consider his influence on other writers. Kennedy asked why Reston didn't like him, and one of his staff people said it wasn't dislike, it was just that he wasn't at ease with Kennedy.

He likes you, I said, turning to John Glenn. He thinks you represent the traditional American values as much as anyone these days. At a dinner party, in 1964, right after Glenn had announced for the Senate, Tom Wicker and I had complained bitterly about him and about the entire glamour syndrome of American politics. So Glenn had walked in space, what did he know about the earth. Was he just one more Kennedy satellite, like Salinger who was now running in California? We were quite strong willed but Reston had defended him. Reston liked the way he talked and what he believed; more, when he landed that day after the space flight and saw his wife for the first time, Reston had caught him "looking first at his Annie, and I liked the look in his eye."

I know, Glenn nodded, I'm having lunch with him in ten days.

The television commentators, Kennedy said, they're the ones. He mentioned a young correspondent covering Mc-Carthy. "Boy, what I wouldn't give to have someone like that on my side." Another aide said yes, and named two other reporters covering McCarthy who were allegedly sympathetic to the McCarthy cause. "They're all doves you know, and because of that they give McCarthy a free ride. Is that fair?" I told Kennedy there were a number of reporters covering him who were sympathetic to him because of his positions on race and Vietnam, and who were treating him a little gently. "You don't expect me to be fair, do you?" he said.

The dinner moved on to a quick discussion of what television would do to politics. There was a general assumption that it would throw the rascals out. "What about the new rascals it throws in?" someone asked, and mentioned Ronald Reagan. A sore point. Kennedy and Reagan had

debated the question of Vietnam on international television
a year before, and the general consensus was that Reagan
had destroyed Kennedy. Part of the trouble had been the
setting; they had answered questions on Vietnam posed by
foreign students, militantly anti-American, and the questions were shrill, angry and hostile. Reagan became the
cool defender of the country, while Kennedy, if he tried to
discuss the substance, looked like he was supporting the
kids. He had been placed in a clearly embarrassing position;
he was off balance and edgy. "Next time you debate him, get
a panel of right-wing kids to ask the questions," someone
said. I dissented: Reagan seemed to me to have memorized
his cards and nothing more, while Kennedy, in contrast,
had tried to answer each question with his own spontaneous
responses, essentially the kind of intelligence and self-
dependence which shows up very well over a long tough
campaign, where automatic cards are not enough. Reagan
had bobbled one question rather badly; a student had asked
him something concerning the Geneva accords. He had
answered smoothly and glibly but had misquoted and
misrepresented the accords, and the kid caught him dead to
rights. He had a copy of the accords right there and had
read it out. It was the kind of mistake which, in a tough
campaign, might be a fatal flaw. A misstep here and the
intense pressure and fatigue of the campaign would magnify it, and the candidate would try and cover up and make
yet another mistake, and soon he would be off balance,
off his natural rhythm. Today an American campaign is a
ruthlessly cruel and searching business; those television
cameras look at you and look back, in Dylan Thomas' words,
"to the bed you were born on." Anyway, I had thought there
were fatal flaws in Reagan. Kennedy agreed and said that I
could judge any future debates between them.

The campaign was a curious, almost contradictory affair. There was no doubt that it was, technically, beginning to go well, that McCarthy was not exactly catching fire though he was running, as usual, a clever campaign that was easily underestimated. (His television was quite good, particularly a last-minute half-hour paid interview with Garry Moore, a real live Hoosier, a local boy, doing the interviewing. It was a slick piece of work, Moore taking the low road, and McCarthy the high road: Senator, isn't it just terrible the way some candidates are spending money? Well Garry, I don't want to comment on that, let's talk about *my* campaign.) As for Branigin, they were sure he'd inevitably diminish as a candidate. Their first polls taken before they entered, the Kennedys always take polls before they enter anything, had shown them tied with Branigin 33–33. But they were convinced that, as the campaign intensified, Branigin, who was playing only to local chauvinism, would fade, the issues in 1968 were simply too great for an Indiana-for-Indianans pitch. They were, of course, building up the Branigin threat, casting themselves as underdogs, a favorite Kennedy trick since the West Virginia primary in 1960 where they poor-mouthed, and poor-mouthed the better to magnify the victory once it was in. The trick, of course, was highly suspect, and when the Kennedys were genuinely pessimistic, as in the last few days of Oregon, the reporters thought they were being put-on.

The problem in Indiana was not so much whether it would be a victory, that looked better and better in late April (though the size was always a question, they wanted fifty percent as a means of ending McCarthy right then and there), but the tone and the balance of the campaign. It had become a curiously contradictory affair, reflecting the changing views of the candidate himself, the changing na-

ture of the country, and the differences among his own advisers. In the beginning, when he had first challenged Johnson, the campaign had been by its very nature new politics
and high-risk politics. It was defying the taboos, it was going outside the party establishment, indeed up against it. Its
main issues were moral ones; it sharpened rather than
muted the differences between Kennedy and the administration. Since the party apparatus was hostile, the campaign's
only resource was shock—quick striking victories, fashioned
on dramatization of the issues, in primary after primary
until California, where a smashing victory would destroy
the President. Though the race was mathematically impossible, it somehow seemed within reach. This was particularly so because one sensed that Johnson was a hollow
man, and when he went, he would go down quickly. While
this phase of the campaign was on, the younger more radical advisers were more in command. They were the shock
troops and they believed in the moral issues and in the
sharpening of them. They had always been the advocates of
the race, because of the preemptive quality of the issues.
They knew little about the delegates, and their strategy was
simple; make the delegates come to you.

Then Johnson withdrew, and a more traditional campaign began. Vietnam disappeared, temporarily at least,
as a viable issue. (In Indiana Kennedy had fumbled around
with it. To raise it as a major issue was considered unpatriotic because of the Paris peace talks, and yet he doubted
the seriousness of these peace talks; indeed the war was the
issue which had forced him into the race.) At the same
time, delegates once locked, even if uneasily, to the President of the United States, became unlocked. "Dick Daley's
office was like a revolving door for Kennedy people for a
few days," said one Chicago politician. The tone of the
campaign had changed, had become muted; the role of the

young radicals, and the other Robert Kennedy people, tempered, much to their annoyance.

Tonight, two weeks after Johnson's withdrawal, Kennedy was on a plane talking with a small group of reporters. The campaign seemed to have gone slack, to have lost its intensity since Johnson pulled out; the quality of spirit, of excitement, almost of a crusade, that had marked the first couple of weeks seemed to have gone. The crowds were noticeably less emotional, and the Kennedy people themselves seemed less spirited; indeed the campaign *was* more cautious. One of the reporters mentioned this and asked Kennedy whether he wished Johnson were back in the race. "No," he said, "it's much better now. It's not as dramatic, and you people [reporters] miss that. Not as exciting. But it's better now. All those delegates are unlocked. The other way was much more exciting but it was more uphill." I disagreed with him; it seemed to me that Johnson's withdrawal had reinstated McCarthy as an important candidate, and that it was going to be much tougher now.

Kennedy started talking about the party. He mentioned the dinner in Philadelphia right after the Johnson withdrawal, an occasion that shattered Walinsky and his colleagues because Kennedy had praised all the old hacks of the party. He said that had he entered New Hampshire against Johnson "there wouldn't be one Democrat in the entire country talking to me. I couldn't have gone to any party dinners at all. They would have booed me. They would all accuse me of dividing the party. Now [because of McCarthy] they know that the division was already there."

Someone mentioned the loyalty of the party people to Johnson, but Kennedy brushed that aside. They were never loyal to Johnson, he said, though they were loyal to the office.

Johnson had been weak with the party, not tending to small party affairs, not going to party dinners ("nobody listens to what you say at them, but it's important to go, important to show that you care"), whereas Humphrey had been very good at tending to party functions. Hubert, he said, had more money in the bank with the pros than Lyndon did. Then he spoke warmly of Humphrey; Humphrey is getting a few breaks, "and if anyone ever deserved a break, he does."

That night, the discussion with several Kennedy aides was about Mayor Daley. (I was writing a piece about Daley when I switched off to cover Kennedy, and I would soon be switching back to the Mayor for a few weeks.) Daley's presence hovered over this entire campaign. Though big city bosses are generally on their way out, he is the last truly powerful one, and though his power is likely to ebb and be diluted nationally in the future, his strength at this convention was immense. He controlled the big Illinois delegation, and some of the smaller bosses with smaller delegations would key on Illinois. This campaign was a curious one, not so much a horse race as a horse show, parading in front of Daley, showing him how much class and style and power you've got, and hoping he agrees. Daley was the judge. Unless the showings in the primaries and the polls were very good, he would probably go to Humphrey, and the Kennedy people were aware of this, aware that Daley was more comfortable with Humphrey than with the more radical, abrasive Kennedy. "One of his other big mistakes in 1968," said Mankiewicz, referring to the failure to enter the race earlier, "is going to be that he thinks Dick Daley regards him in the same light that he regarded Jack Kennedy. It's a very different time now."

There was general agreement about this, for this was a group of the newer Kennedy people. Someone noted the enormous difference in styles and worlds of Daley and

Kennedy. When Kennedy was trying to decide whether or not to enter the race, he made one rather odd last-minute attempt to maneuver Johnson on the war; he proposed an objective panel on the war which would recommend ways of getting out with honor. The White House leaked word of this to reporters. Kennedy was enraged, and called Daley, asking him for advice about what to do. Daley's advice was immediate: Just deny it. "Can you imagine that," said the Kennedy man, "there's Bob with forty of the most important reporters in the country waiting outside his hotel door, and the White House has already leaked it—a pretty official damn leak—and Daley says, *deny it*. Cook County is a long way from modern politics."

There was a general assumption that Kennedy was to have a much tougher time ahead with Daley than he realized, that a coolness existed which the Senator had not realized. ("What hotel is Bob Kennedy taking over in Chicago?" a reporter asked a Daley aide in late April, and the Daley man answered, "Bobby Kennedy isn't taking over anything in this city.") The one thing working for Kennedy was that despite Daley's probable preference for Humphrey, he likes winners above all, that's why he had steadily expanded his power base, and the Kennedy people believed that they could prove that they had the winner and that Humphrey simply couldn't carry a weak ticket. One Kennedy man recalled being in Chicago with Jack Kennedy in 1960, at the time of the debates, when Daley was actively for Kennedy. "Jack arrived and was preparing for the debate and he kept asking us, 'Where's Daley? Where's Daley? Anybody heard from Daley?' And no Daley of course. So we had the debate, and the moment it was over, who's the first guy bursting into the television studios, surrounded by a phalanx of his yes-men? Why Daley of course. He knew for the first time he'd got a *winner*."

Kennedy became more dependent on the traditionalists who had opposed the race but were now more at ease with it. They knew delegates, they worked among the delegates, but they also were a tempering influence on the campaign. The delegates, many of whom were tied to the big city machines, were uneasy with Kennedy's radicalism and his ties to Negroes. In Chicago, for instance, the militant blacks Kennedy had touched were the sworn enemies of Daley and his machine. Daley was uneasy with Kennedy's appeals; if this young man were elected he might threaten the city machine. He might give federal money directly to these wild black men, and thus cut off the machine's power among the poor blacks through traditional patronage. He might just finance Dick Daley's opposition, and Daley was not happy about the course of it. And Daley might now be the most important single man in the party. And so the delegates were uneasy with the course of the campaign. A basic split soon developed between the radicals, the Robert Kennedy people, and the traditionalists or Jack Kennedy people, with someone like Fred Dutton serving vaguely in the middle as an interpreter to the generations. "The young people think the New Politics is already here and they want Bob to lead it in, or failing that, to be a martyr to it," said one staff man. "What they don't see is that Bob is a transitional figure with ties to both the new and the old, but that he also wants very much to win. They have too much conviction. They are too sure of themselves for the complexities and pluralism of American politics. Walinsky makes too many flat statements such as 'the country is against the war,' or 'the country is for the Negro.' The kind of thing they want Bob to do is the sort of thing you do from the pulpit or from the editorial page, but not necessarily in politics. They want something new, the sharpening of issues and differences. You could almost call it the politics of abrasiveness. The traditionalists want to soften the differences, ease them over, say something like there's no real difference here between you and me, but our guy is better and besides, he's a winner."

The young radicals for their part thought that the cutback on race ("I was the chief law enforcement of this country . . .") was a mistake, morally and politically. The entire country already knew where Kennedy stood on the race issue, particularly those who hated Negroes. There was no sense in 1968, with its instant communications, of trying to fool them. Those who hated Negroes would know where Robert Kennedy stood—either they would hate him too, or they would come aboard. But cutting back was harmful among the liberals with whom he was in already serious trouble. His image was blurred. If national reporters and television reflected his edginess on race, as they were bound to and as they did, then it would hurt him once more there. It would re-create the image of the too political Bobby, and this finally would backfire. (What is the difference between you and Barry Goldwater on some of these programs in the ghetto—about plans to involve the private sector more in the cities, he was once asked. "The difference is that I mean it," he answered.) The view, expressed by Walinsky, was "we should do our own thing, and win and then let the delegates come to us." The young men were still bitter about the failure to enter the race the previous fall ("We'd have the nomination by now," one said in late April), about the loss of their real base to McCarthy—the professors, liberals, intellectuals, kids. They thought that this had thrown Kennedy off balance in the campaign. Because he had come in late, McCarthy had picked up Kennedy's natural base and as a result Kennedy was forced to appeal to blue-collar people, which contradicted his appeal to blacks and liberals. Had he entered early he would have been right on balance, running from strength with Negroes, kids and liberals, and pitching to blue collar simply by his presence. He would have been able to go into working-class neighborhoods and instead of talking about law enforcement, he could talk from a stronger position, putting the emphasis on the need for generosity, and reconciliation in America.

There was an additional problem here; Robert Kennedy's course had been one of the traditional politician turning toward an increasingly radical position. In the process, men like Walinsky had played a considerable role. They always felt that it was an uphill one: softening your real advice on three out of four positions so that you did not look too much like a radical, and so that you looked like you had good common sense, were a professional, and then slipping in your advice on the fourth point. Now the young aides saw other men coming up and using what they considered to be self-serving conservatism: trimming on what they really felt in order to ingratiate themselves. "You-know-I'm-liberal-myself,-but-is-the-country-really-ready-for-this." The younger men regarded Sorensen as the arch enemy; they had looked to Richard Goodwin, though he had served in the earlier administration, as a soul brother. (Goodwin, was a swing figure politically. After having run some shabby errands for Johnson on the war, he had become deeply involved with the opposition to it. Of all the Kennedy people, he alone had gone to work for McCarthy—showing up in New Hampshire and telling Seymour Hersh, McCarthy's then press secretary, "Just you and me, Sy, and one typewriter, and we're going to bring down the President of the United States." When he finally came back to Kennedy, after Wisconsin, he called the candidate and made sure he realized that it was not Gene McCarthy or Bob Kennedy who had brought Lyndon Johnson down, but Dick Goodwin.

It was a call which delighted Kennedy with its egocentrism.) But Goodwin, after joining the Kennedy campaign, had busied himself becoming Kennedy's television expert, and had participated to a limited degree in ideological conflicts. Indeed some of the other staffers felt that Goodwin seemed a little unsure of himself in the Kennedy camp, as though he felt he might be a little distrusted for his prior service in the enemy camp. The radicals' best friend in court was the candidate himself, and they felt he had surrounded himself with too many men who were now viewed as professionals, whereas they were viewed only as amateurs.

Thus the uneven and at times contradictory tone of the campaign. The formal tone was constricted but then again and again the passion would break through, in question-and-answer sessions, where the candidate would react, more often than not, to the smugness and complacency of white America. It would jar him out of his own nervousness. One of the most poignant examples was at Purdue. It was a conservative audience, not with him at the beginning, during his dull speech. But then, during the question-and-answer period, he began to talk about the poor in America, about what it was like to grow up with rats in Bedford Stuyvesant, how the schools maim, what it was like to be in an Indian school and read only the white man's characterization of Indian life. Finally there was a deep and moving description of the disenfranchised in America: ". . . the almost impassable barriers between the poor and the rest of the country." It won a prolonged standing ovation from the audience, converted several otherwise critical reporters, and led one Washington columnist to say, "Scotty Reston always claimed that Jack Kennedy never educated the people on their country, but you've just seen as good an example of it as you'll see in American politics."

Probably the best example of the passion and the anger came in late April when Kennedy met with medical students at Indiana University. It is a fact of American life that the medical profession has become a hard core of American conservatism. In 1964, as I traveled with Goldwater, the hard core of the committee at those $100 a plate dinners was doctors, and here at Indianapolis they were in their embryo stage, the new young conservatives, Reagan country. (One looked at them and listened to their questions and recalled a great Goldwater rally in suburban Chicago in 1964, and the very posh teen-age children going around in their Madras sports jackets with huge signs saying "We Want Freedom.") The hall was packed and, for a Kennedy audience, markedly reserved. In the balcony, a Negro, obviously a maintenance man, shouted "We want Kennedy." Immediately about a dozen others, all students, shouted back "oh no we don't."

"Some of my people," he began, "have been trying to organize a committee of doctors for Kennedy in Indiana. And they're still trying." Mild applause. Then the speech, strong but not terribly well done, an indictment of U.S. medical programs. We are lagging behind other countries, and twelve other nations, "some of them Communist," have a higher life-expectancy rate than the U.S.; a call for the restructuring of American medical care, which included expanded programs and greater decentralization of decision making. When he finished, the applause was polite. Then a flood of questions, almost all conservative, almost all dubious and hostile. Where would the money come from, someone asked. "The federal govement will have to make some available," he said. "Money implies control," a student shouted. "Barry Goldwater lost that struggle four years ago," he said. It went on, and finally, angry now, angry at the smugness, he said, "The fact is there are people who suffer in this country and some of the rest of us have a responsibility. I look around me here and I don't see many black faces. Frankly, the poor have difficulty entering your profession. You can say that the federal government does this or fails here or doesn't do that, but it is really our society that is responsible. That there are more rats than people in New York is intolerable; after all, the poor are the ones who are doing most of the fighting in Vietnam, while white students sit here in medical school."

With that they began to hiss and boo, and they began to shout, "We're going, we're going, we've signed up."

"Oh yes," he said, "going there sometime in the future. It's not the same thing. The dying is going on now, *right now,* while we're talking." What about college deferments? someone shouted; he was against them. What about medical school deferments, are you against them? "Well, the way things are going here, I guess the answer is yes. I don't want to say anything you might approve of."

Later, on the plane, he kept shaking his head about the afternoon. "They were so comfortable," he said, "so comfortable. Didn't you think they were comfortable?"

Election night. The old excitement. The hotel filled with all the team: faces from the past, new faces, the good looking Kennedy women with their expensive coats (you can always recognize the rich women because they put money into their coats a non-political expert told me). A buoyant atmosphere, and the feeling that Kennedy will go to about forty-five percent and the hope that McCarthy will be disposed of, so that they can get on with the business at hand—Hubert. Early returns were very good. The Negroes were coming in just fine. One black precinct which John Kraft, the pollster, had told them to look for came in: Branigin 16, McCarthy 52, Kennedy 697. "I think that's my favorite precinct," said Mankiewicz. Winners' words, winners' smiles. The Poles in Gary came through, 2-to-1, despite the machine. More smiles. A Negro ward came in and it had Kennedy over Branigin by only 166 to 102. Someone complained about it. "There's nothing wrong with that total," said Larry O'Brien, "I would say that the regular organization is functioning effectively in that ward. They had the foresight to bring whiskey." Winners' words again. The lead seemed to be about 45-to-26-to-26. The television sets were all on that afternoon and one TV newscaster said that Kennedy's showing was disappointing. "Disappointing to who," said Tuck, "not to you, you sonofabitch, you never liked us anyway." (Later that night, a reporter, wandering through the crowd, picked up a TV broadcaster and pleaded with his home office. "Yes, yes I know the other networks have had him on, and have interviewed him, but Tuck refuses to let him go on with us until we pronounce him a winner. You declare him a winner and I'll get him on. It's that damn Tuck.") McCarthy, on the television, was saying that it wasn't a defeat. "Well, I don't know," Kennedy said, "I don't know whether people think it's so good to be second or third. That's not the way I was brought up. I always was taught that it's much better to win." He was laughing. "I learned that when I was about two." It was coming on, not exactly what they had wanted, they had wanted that fifty, but it was forty-two in a conservative state and with a rushed-up campaign, and they had those Slav wards, 2-to-1; a fine gift for the omnipresent Mayor Daley. Larry O'Brien was already on the television spreading the sweet syrup; how happy they were, how they had come into Indiana and run against such a fine popular governor like Roger Branigin, and they were pleased to do so well against such difficult odds. And it had been a fine campaign, a clean one, and Roger Branigin, well, he was a fine governor, imagine beating him here in Indiana. Adam Walinsky wanted to issue a statement calling the returns a victory for social justice. Someone told him, no Adam, not this time.

And the candidate? He was celebrating by having dinner with two intense young McCarthy workers whom he had found, dispirited, in the lobby. They were still a little bitter and they complained about the quality of Kennedy's young people, and the fact that when they went into the ghettos none of the Negroes would listen to them. Kennedy suggested that perhaps McCarthy hadn't worked hard enough in the ghettos.

"But you're a Kennedy," the girl said. "It sounds like a newspaper rehash, but it still is right. You have the name."

"Look," he said, "I agree I have a tremendous advantage with my last name. But let me ask you why can't McCarthy go into a ghetto? Why can't he go into a poor neighborhood? Can you tell me when he's been involved in those areas?"

"You've got a tremendous headstart in those areas," the girl insisted. "But he was there first on the war. He declared himself first."

And with that, Indiana was finished.

III

He was an odd and beguiling figure. Patrick Anderson had once written that Robert Kennedy was not a simple man, but many simple men; a good description. His reputation was for ruthlessness, yet in 1968, there was no major political figure whose image so contrasted with the reality. Part of it was simply the quality of change. He was a man of constant growth and change, and while journalistic stereotypes are, more often than not, accurate as long as the person involved stands still, they are likely to be several years out of date if he changes as much as Kennedy did. Most politicians seem somewhat attractive from a distance, but under closer examination they fade: the pettiness, the vanities, the little vulgarities come out. This was to hurt McCarthy as the campaign progressed, for some of the young people who worked most directly with him would find some of their enthusiasm dimmed by his lack of generosity, his cool, almost arrogant, introversion. Robert Kennedy was different. Under closer examination he was far more winning than most, with little bitterness or pettiness. For in those days, if one was a Kennedy there was little reason to feel embittered or cheated. There was little false vanity or false modesty because, as a Kennedy, the action swirled around him; he was automatically at the center of things. Even when a Kennedy is out of power his telephone still rings. He seemed like the other Kennedys, still a fresh figure in our politics, which in some measure was a benefit of his wealth. For it is true that having money as a national politician is not so important as *not* having money. There is a gradual erosion to a politician who lacks wealth—too many years attending too many dinners, asking too many rich men favors, listening to their inanities and then thanking them. Kennedys and Rockefellers are spared that. He was intelligent and knowledgeable about the world; indeed there was now no one in his entourage who knew more of the world. This too was indicative of the change of the past few years; for there were men who had once been major intellectual influences on his brother, who had taught the Kennedys about America and about the world. But Robert Kennedy had passed them by now. There might be people who knew more about one particular country, but none who knew as much about as many things. He had traveled too much, been briefed too often by very able people; he had access again and again to the most powerful and informed people in the world. His was the best education a rich family and a powerful nation could provide. He was quick to admit his own mistakes (the only major figure who had been involved in Vietnam to have done so; a fine index of the intellectual integrity of our times), and curiously fatalistic about himself, for if one is a Kennedy there is a sense that it can all be achieved, but also that it can all be snatched away.

Thus again and again, during the campaign, reporters would ask him what his long range plans were, and he would answer that you never really knew; you lived day to day; it was all like Russian roulette. He could talk with striking detachment about his own career (though not about John Kennedy's, that was still emotional. One could easily criticize anything Robert Kennedy had done in his lifetime, but one did not criticize aspects of Jack Kennedy's career without quickly and sharply changing the tone of the conversation; his voice getting a little icier, the eyes getting a little harder). He could sit one night and talk fatalistically about Indiana, on the eve of the primary, about the people, they had given him at least a fair chance, about the people who hated him in the state, the transplanted Kentuckians, and Tennesseans, out of place, scared for their jobs, scared by the Negroes, scared by Robert Kennedy. Sometimes, he had said that night, you could feel them hate straight at you. "I can understand that." As for the kids working for McCarthy who hated him, he understood that too. He probably would feel exactly the same if he were one of them; but they were good, weren't they? What he wouldn't give to have them on his side. McCarthy had the A kids, the best of them, and that was hard to take. They'll come back some day, someone said. He answered, Oh, perhaps eventually, but it will probably never be the same thing. They may never forgive themselves or me for making it happen.

His sense of humor was very good in small groups and he could be very funny. Yet he often seemed ill at ease in his public appearances, and he performed worst in a sterile television studio without any audience. He performed best under intense critical, indeed emotional, circumstances and under heckling. In public he would be cool toward a business group, unless they were so smug that he was angered, and he would spend long hours with a young people's group or with Negroes. (Nevertheless, he could, on occasion, flash moments of almost absent-minded rudeness for such a normally sensitive man. A reporter traveling in upstate New York in early 1968 would come across a pleasant congenial Democratic functionary who hated Robert Kennedy with a very special passion. The reason was simple. In 1964 he had driven Kennedy around his section of the state in his own car. Kennedy had sat in the front seat and said to him snappishly, "Turn off the heater!" The driver had done nothing, waited ten minutes, and then, "It's a little warm in here, would you like the heater turned down, Mister Kennedy?" Kennedy had answered, "Yes, please.") Conversation with him was never particularly easy, and he was often abrupt. A reporter did not really interview him; at best he talked his way through with him, not so much asking questions as proffering ideas and judging his reactions. "You have to learn to read the pauses," his former press secretary Ed Guthman once said of him. Young radicals uneasy and distrusting of him would find him interested in their ideas and willing to listen at great length. High ranking labor leaders expecting to tell him about their demands on minimum wage might find themselves questioned sharply, even rudely, on what they were doing to end discrimination in their unions. He lacked Jack Kennedy's absolute confidence in himself and his charm, and most important, his confidence that he could project that charm. "More than any man I ever knew," John Kenneth Galbraith once said of Jack Kennedy, he "liked being himself and was at ease with himself." The people around Robert Kennedy were regularly telling him to loosen up, but it did not come easily: his knuckles would be cracking away, his hands wrestling with each other—he was not a loose man. He was less graceful and more committed than his brother.

Kennedy had the dual advantage of being rich, which gave him one kind of asset, and of coming from a home where the Anglo-Saxon prejudice against the Irish had generated a rage to succeed and to excel, and which would prevent the squandering of money. The Kennedys would not let their money distort or soften them. They would dominate the money; the money would not dominate them. They understood, as few wealthy families in this country understood, its advantages and its liabilities. Joe Kennedy, said a contemporary, "is sort of like a caterpillar. He couldn't

quite become a butterfly, but his boys were going to fly, no
matter what." Robert came from way down the list of children, the seventh of nine ("When you come from that far
down you have to struggle to survive," he later said). He was
by far the smallest of the boys and in a family in which there
was a relentless success cult, his lack of size drove him
even harder. That, and the fact that he came along at the
tail end of World War II, and always felt a strong sense
of disappointment at not having seen combat, were frustrations which drove him even harder in the postwar years. He
did not learn much at college but he learned from his personal experience. As his life touched things in the outside
world, he would become interested in them. He had had, as
a young man, a special quality which would later set him
apart from most men in public life: that indignation, an
almost primitive and innocent anger—that things were
not what they should be or were supposed to be. Had he
not had the wealth and family position which springboarded
him into immediate public service, he might either have
lost this indignation through the erosion of a thousand
smaller deals and battles at a lower level, or his very intensity might have blocked out a public career, for men that intense are not always trusted by their peers; they are often
considered extremist, in the American vernacular. But because of his family he was able both to enter public life at a
very high level and retain that intensity.

In his public career, that outrage was turned at first
to relatively minor issues, indeed sometimes to the wrong
issues. But as he became a full-fledged public servant, he
turned it to the great and dark questions of American life.
This quality took him to stands and causes far beyond those
accepted by more traditional liberals who accepted the society at face value. At dinner late one night in Indiana, Kennedy and Bill Haddad, an ex-newspaperman who had also

served in the Peace Corps and the poverty program, and I
were talking about the campaign. It seemed to me, I said,
that as the campaign developed it was taking Kennedy further and further outside the establishment; that the more he
saw of the country, the more he was turned off by the establishment and the existing representatives of existing institutions, and the more he was involved with the poor. (Indeed,
Dick Harwood of *The Washington Post* would a month later
write an incisive story pointing out that Kennedy had earlier
said McCarthy faced the danger of being a one-issue man
on Vietnam, but now Kennedy himself, tied to the poor, was
sounding like a one-issue man.) Yes, Kennedy said, it was
pointless to talk about the problem in America being black
and white, it was really rich and poor, which was a much
more complex subject. But if you keep going this way, I
asked, won't you finally have to take on the establishment.
Kennedy nodded. And what if you take over and find that the
very institutions of government and the society are stran-
gling the country and perpetuating the imbalance? Haddad
asked him. "Then we will have to change the institutions,"
he answered quietly. Then he began to talk about the problems that would be involved in changing the institutions in
this country non-violently. Haddad looked over at me as
if this were a signal victory. Many months afterward he said
that this was the first moment when he was convinced that
Kennedy was different from other politicians and that he
was the one major political figure who understood where
everything was going and how serious it was. "He was willing to change the institutions. Even John Kennedy didn't
go that far. John Kennedy's instinct, when he ran up against
the institutions, was to try and challenge them, to elevate
them. Which worked a little, but really didn't work. Before,
when I was in the Peace Corps and things would go wrong,
I'd go running over to the White House and scream at Kenny

O'Donnell. 'You think you run the country! You don't even run it from here to across the street!' and he would answer 'The trouble with you Haddad is that you think we don't know it.' And now here was Bob, seeing how deep it went, and how bad it was, and then suddenly breaking through— it was like finally seeing the blue sky. You had a sense he could go all the way and do something about it."

He could bring into American politics some of the very best people in the game: fresh, intelligent, even joyous men of a variety of views, and he could inspire them to an extraordinary degree. That was in part because he did not like sycophants, and because, more than most strong men who like power, he could listen to the quiet dissenting voices. Indeed one of the better epitaphs might have later read that, in a time of growing pessimism about American life among many of the best-informed young men, Robert Kennedy had nonetheless served as a rallying point for many of the most talented young men of the nation; men who were scarred by the events of the past decade, but still saw, through him, a hope of turning the country around. Yet he could also tolerate, on the fringes, self-serving and frivolous people; so that to the outsider, the Robert Kennedy people were blurred. Was it Fred Dutton, a rare practicing intellectual in American politics, or Mankiewicz, the thoughtful press secretary, who had decided to work for Kennedy when the Senator had denounced the government's refusal of burial privileges to Robert Thompson, a Distinguished Service Medal winner but also an ex-member of the Communist party? Or was it John Lewis, the former head of Snick, a poor Negro boy from Troy, Alabama, still hopeful that the American dream might work, or was it some silly socialite? I remember once being in a crowd of some of his young social friends and wondering how in God's name he could tolerate them, and deciding there must be some mean, perverse little Irish

quirk in Kennedy which permitted him to accept the fawn-
ing of these people: one more victory for his family.

He was visualized as a total politician, yet he frequently did things which were, technically at least, bad
politics. His championing of the California grape pickers
was, at best, high-risk politics and, by traditional standards,
bad politics. One makes powerful enemies for marginally
effective friends. His constant reiteration about the plight
of the American Indians, their suicide rate, their hopelessness, had little impact on a crisis-belching American middle
class which can accept no more than two causes at a given
time.

He had become the chief spokesman of the dispossessed
in this country and, God knows, the conservatives and reac-
tionaries knew it. (In Texas, it was virtually impossible to
get anyone to work for him in 1968. Someone finally asked
Judge Woodrow Wilson Bean, one of the few men openly
supporting Kennedy, why he was doing it, and Bean answered: "Because if he's elected, anyone from Texas will
need a pass to get into Washington, and I'm going to be the
man handing out the passes.") Yet, as he started his race,
he was distrusted by liberals and intellectuals to a surprising
degree. People who felt deeply about his brother regarded
him with grave misgivings and deep suspicion, though in
1968 he had a far greater proven record than Jack Kennedy
had in 1960.

Part of it was that he was a Kennedy, which meant
that everything was bigger than life. He could not be judged
like other men; more had been given to him, more was expected of him, and more would be doubted about him. In
Indiana, for example, he had attracted a much bigger press
corps because he was a Kennedy, but similarly, when he
won, a striking victory in a conservative state, he got surprisingly little credit for his victory. Only a landslide or a

defeat would move the press. Indeed *The New York Times*
and two of the networks called McCarthy the big winner in
Indiana, because he had not been eliminated. The other part
of it was the Kennedys' own fault. Like the rest of us, they
wanted things both ways but unlike the rest of us, they more
often than not had it both ways. They wanted to be able to
complain about the lack of privacy given them by the press,
and yet be able to summon photographers and reporters
from important magazines to reveal all kinds of innermost
thoughts at opportune moments and permit all kinds of
spontaneous family photographs. They wanted to be able
to get the full measure and mileage out of the power and
unity of the family, to the degree that outsiders felt that the
power thrust of the family came first and issues second, and
yet they wanted, at the same time, to convince the uneasy,
sophisticated dissenter that they were doing all these things
because of the issues involved. Then there was Camelot.
The country at times liked Kennedy for being part of Camelot, and then hated him because of course there was no
Camelot. And why did the Kennedys pretend there was?
Wasn't it nice to have an American royal family at last,
but who were these Kennedys, did they think they were
better than the rest of us?

Thus he could not be like other men and this feeling
extended to all of us; we all had our ambivalent feelings
about him. I remember the night of Martin Luther King's
funeral. I sat with Jack Nelson of the *Los Angeles Times,*
one of the most distinguished reporters in the country, a
strong idealistic man, and perhaps as knowledgeable about
race in the South as any man in the country, and a fan of
Kennedy's. We were talking about the long, grueling march
in the very hot weather from the church to Morehouse College. Kennedy had made the march and had evoked by far
the most passionate response from Negroes along the way.

Yet he had taken off his jacket, as had some others, and I was complaining about this. I suppose I felt it was half youth-cult and half tough-cult, but Nelson was defending him. Others had taken their coats off; it was only normal; it was not demagogic. Why, he said, Martin Luther King would have taken off his coat at the funeral. No he wouldn't, I said, you just don't do that. No, said Nelson, King had even done it, at the funeral of Jimmie Lee Jackson, but when Kennedy does it, you all read too much into it. Case closed.

Yet finally when he was judged, he had to be judged not just on the past and the mythology of the past, but in his time, when America itself was changing so rapidly, and on his capacity for growth. They were not just the years before the White House, or even the three years in power, as the right hand of The Man, but also and equally important, those post-power years when he had stood outside the power establishment looking in, and had become consumed by the poor in America, and the inequities within the system. He had changed radically and he understood the rapid changes in America, and this did not always help him. Not only were many of the reporters describing the early Robert Kennedy, but they were also writing about their own version of America—vintage 1960. One man, Bill Wilson, a talented young television producer, an early Stevensonian, had worked with Jack Kennedy in 1960. He had not liked Robert Kennedy and had reluctantly come to work for him in 1968, but was startled by the change; "Now he is tough of mind and tough of spirit, not just tough of mouth."

Kennedy had begun his public career as a social illiterate. He worked for a time for the justice department, and then took a job with the McCarthy committee, a natural enough liaison worked out through his father, who admired Mc-

Carthy. (McCarthy and the elder Kennedy had become good friends; the elder Kennedy admired McCarthy for his enemies: liberals, members of the Eastern establishment, and the British.) Kennedy's role was not major, largely working out statistics on allies who were trading with the Communists during the Korean war, and he eventually ended up as a counsel for the Democrats on the committee. He admired McCarthy, did not dissent or even think to dissent from what he was doing. He did not see anything particularly destructive to it, and saw McCarthy being destroyed by Roy Cohn and David Schine who played to his desire for publicity. ("He was on a toboggan," he would later tell one interviewer. "It was so exciting and exhilarating as he went downhill that it didn't matter to him if he hit a tree at the bottom. Cohn and Schine took him up the mountain and showed him all those wonderful things. He destroyed himself for that—for publicity.") Kennedy broke with McCarthy more over Roy Cohn than anything else; a relationship which almost ended with a fistfight. He ended his tour of the McCarthy committee by serving as counsel for the Democrats, though he did remain loyal to McCarthy to the end, one of the few who did, as the Wisconsin Senator ravaged himself. At the end, Kennedy received an award as one of the Junior Chamber of Commerce's young men of the year but walked out during the main speech by Edward R. Murrow, who had distinguished himself to most of the nation by his battles with McCarthy.

After that he joined the Senate Rackets Committee, becoming a relentless chaser of hoods in general and Jimmy Hoffa in particular. Here the full force of his indignation was felt for the first time in this country. One reporter who covered the Teamster investigations was enormously impressed with Kennedy's determination, his single-mindedness, the way his anger exploded at Hoffa's operation and

Hoffa's belief that he was beyond American laws. "At once you admired what he was doing, the intensity of it all, and how well he did it, and at the same time you wondered a little about Kennedy and how he felt about labor in general," the reporter said. This was a feeling that much of labor's leadership was to retain; the leadership went for Jack Kennedy in 1960, but it always remained uneasy about Robert Kennedy. It felt that he had enjoyed the Hoffa prosecution a little too much, and this hurt him some in 1968. Kennedy's puritanism bloomed and flourished during the combat with the hoods and the toughs. Joe Gallo, one of the hoods investigated, later recalled that Kennedy had looked at him and said, " 'So you're Joe Gallo the Jukebox. You don't look so tough. I'd like to fight you myself.' So I hadda tell him I don't fight." Kennedy himself thought that the toughs, themselves, were overrated. He once told a friend that anyone who talked as much about being tough as Hoffa did, couldn't really be that tough. Yet a violent struggle emerged; they threatened each other, they swapped insults, they were ready to match each other in push-ups. Kennedy once drove home past midnight, the last person to leave the Senate office building, only to see the lights in Hoffa's Teamster office still on; he turned around and went back to his own office. Kennedy was in those days very much the prosecutor, not a great social-cause-and-effect man. He saw the American system working, and working well, and he simply saw Hoffa violating it. The Teamster years were not beneficial for him. Rather they benefitted Jack Kennedy, giving him needed national exposure, and hurt Robert Kennedy's standing with his future constituents, the liberals. He did, however, make some acquaintances among the extraordinary group of investigative reporters covering the Teamsters who were to become his most trusted friends: Wally Turner, John Seigenthaler, Ed Guthman. Yet Kennedy would retain, and find difficult to shake, the image of a prosecutor, and people in general, and liberals in particular, do not like prosecutors. Liberals do not like investigations of labor, even if it is corrupt. In those days it went against their instincts, it might be labor baiting, and yes, they would think, maybe Hoffa is abusive, but isn't he being singled out? In sum, Kennedy would lose more by the Hoffa investigation than he would gain. Hoffa would call him ruthless, and that would stick. Hoffa might be ruthless too, but he would not be running one day for the presidency of the United States.

He had never, of course, lost sight of the priority assignment in those days—to elect Jack Kennedy President. That ambition was the family ambition and it never dimmed. Was Seigenthaler a close friend through the Rackets Committee investigations? Well then, the Kennedys would later send Robert down to Nashville and use that connection as a base in searching for delegates, in meeting people. In 1956 they had an attractive young candidate, and they had come within a hair of the vice-presidency in the open convention. Beaten by Kefauver, Robert Kennedy, working the floor, had found that many delegates liked Jack Kennedy, thought him a real comer, but Estes, well old Estes had been to their homes, had sent them postcards. Between 1956 and 1960 a lot of postcards were sent out by the Kennedys and a lot of homes visited. (Jet travel has enormously changed political conventions. In the old days when travel was so slow, the proselytizing was done at the conventions and thus the delegates arrived more malleable. Now, with jets, they are visited, wined and dined locally and sought at their very doorsteps. By convention time one nominally knows whom they're for.) The interim years were thus crucial and the Kennedys became adept at all this; there were so many of them to go visiting and they always had the financial resources to do it. But the 1956 race proved valuable. Young Robert Kennedy traveled with the Stevenson campaign all over the country, sitting quietly, realizing that the election was lost, but that it was a fortuitous break that Kefauver rather than his brother was on the ticket (the onus would not go against the Catholics). He made endless notes on how badly the campaign was run, the poor timing, the waste of the candidate's time and energy, the failure to schedule well, the lack of press kits.

He was an excellent campaign manager for his brother in 1960. Though it was Jack Kennedy's campaign, an extraordinary number of the key men, the organizers, the drivers, were men brought in by Robert. It was as if Jack were in charge of the intellectual component, the speeches, the policies, the ideology, while Robert was in charge of organizing, of the talent, of the *loyalty*, picking and deciding which men could do it and which could not. Bobby would test the men; Jack would test the ideas. As campaign manager he had the total trust of his brother. He guarded Jack's interest zealously; Jack was a precious commodity and was not to be scratched, worn down or irritated. He understood Jack and his best interests. The brothers, different in style and in friends, had been brought much closer by politics; without the common link of Jack's destiny, they might have gone quite different ways, with different friends, different wives, different tastes. Now Jack Kennedy had a campaign manager who understood not only the candidate, but the family; someone who would not be too independent, or seek his own publicity, or get independent ideas, and someone who could take the heat. This latter is terribly important.

A campaign is a difficult thing and there are endless decisions to be made. Not only must the candidate be saved from making them in order to conserve his time, but more—

a lot of the decisions are cruel, they have an element of rejection in them, and they can make enemies. Thus a person whose campaign idea or campaign role is rejected must not be made to think that it was the candidate who had turned him down. He must think that it was unsympathetic underlings. In this case it was the illiberal Bobby who was blocking him out. It was also Bobby who had to separate the endless fights between the local reform groups and the local machines, while keeping both in the Kennedy camp. It must always be the Good Jack and the Bad Bobby. "I'm not running a popularity contest," he said at the time. "It doesn't matter if people like me or not. Jack can be nice to them. I don't try to antagonize people, but somebody has to be able to say No. If people are not getting off their behinds, how do you say that?" He was very good, always willing to take the heat, always willing to back up his people, and willing to try the unorthodox. (A young political science professor who bucked the organization in upstate New York, in 1960, got an enormous kickback from the machine, which went directly to Robert Kennedy: Was one young egghead worth five old professionals, even if Kennedy himself had given the go ahead on the strategy earlier? The professor, to his surprise, found that Kennedy backed him up. He became a lifelong and influential devotee.) Kennedy was at times rough and almost too devoted to his purpose. Anyone, in those simplistic days, who opposed Jack was a bad guy likely to be roughly treated; and even friends found their sensibilities trampled on. A lifetime of intelligent and dedicated service to certain principles meant nothing to Kennedy if the person was somehow blocking, or likely to help block, Jack Kennedy's presidential ambitions. Harsh words were spoken; and years later people would exonerate Jack Kennedy and remember Bobby Kennedy. It was at the convention that he told the unhappy Humphrey, wavering between Stevenson and Kennedy, "Hubert, we want your announcement and the pledge of the Minnesota delegation today or else." To which Humphrey replied: "Go to hell." But he ran an excellent campaign. They had enough delegates, and they kept them in line. If he was frequently and justifiably accused of twisting arms one notch too many, it was also true that on the first ballot their calculations were almost letter perfect. It was also true that the first ballot was vital. The bosses still had their doubts about Kennedy and the liberals still loved Stevenson, and any defection might start an outbound tide. If they missed on the first ballot, they might miss completely. But the convention was won, and so was the campaign. Jack became the handsome young President and Robert took the heat; he had won for his brother but lost for himself.

If it is not traditional to appoint the campaign manager Attorney General, it is not exactly unusual either. So the question very early became whether Jack would appoint Robert to the justice department. The President was reluctantly inclined toward it, he wanted Robert Kennedy around and he trusted his advice. Joseph Kennedy was enthusiastically for it; the cries of dynasty hardly frightened or embarrassed him. Nothing would have pleased him more than to have founded a dynasty. Robert himself was dubious. He remembered that when Nixon had visited South Carolina during the 1960 campaign, Bill Rogers, the Attorney General and one of the ablest members of the Eisenhower administration, had been forced to hide in the plane because of his unpopularity. (Eight years later Robert Kennedy, visiting Atlanta, would see a young girl named Kathy McGrath, a twenty-two-year-old secretary who had come to the airport to meet him. When she asked for his autograph he would write: "To Kathy. You are now in charge of my campaign in Georgia. Good luck. You'll need it. Bob Kennedy.") Besides, there were other things in the administration which he would have liked to try, perhaps in State or Defense, places where he could learn and could soften the intensity of feeling against him. Jack Kennedy, wanting his brother in this special role, finally decided to go ahead, though noting to a friend: "I'd like to open the door at about 3 A.M. and announce that Bobby is the Attorney General and then shut the door and run like hell." Jack Kennedy, witty, gracious, charming, had always been amused by his younger brother's ability to take the heat for him. In 1962 a group of congressmen dropped by the White House to pay the President a visit. It was a pleasant amiable session and finally one Southern congressman said, "Mister President, I'm afraid I'm going to have to attack you in a speech for all this civil-rights activity." The President laughed and said: "Why can't you just call Bobby a son of a bitch?"

The early days of the John Kennedy administration were marked by a certain arrogance of the hard-nosed— we're eggheads, but we're tough too—and Robert Kennedy was one of the leading offenders. It was a time when activist eggheads with muscles were in, and old soft eggheads, many of them Stevensonians, were out. The newer men were in their late thirties and early forties, more often than not combat veterans of the war, well-read, articulate, playing down their idealism; it was not something one talked about. Chester Bowles was almost symbolic of the old kind, though many of the administration's best ambassadorial appointments were made by him. He was too avowedly liberal, too quick to talk openly, in daily conversation, about idealism. Robert Kennedy was to finally emerge, in instance after instance, as the single most important liberal influence in the administration, but the very idea of this would have

appalled him. In those days he would have been embarrassed to go around spouting liberal ideology; his liberalism
was camouflaged under the tough-guy exterior. When
Bowles appeared ready to blab about having been against
the Bay of Pigs, Robert Kennedy's finger went into his
stomach: *you were for it, remember that.* (The story went
around the country and it wasn't the Bowles people who
put it out either.) Indeed part of the mystique of the administration was toughness—Floyd Patterson's photograph
hung in the Attorney General's office until Patterson lost
the heavyweight title. Shortly after the administration
started, with speaking invitations coming in from everywhere and very few being accepted, one came in from a
Polish group. Come on, he said, let's take that one. I like
the Poles, they're tough.

When Burke Marshall was being looked over for Assistant Attorney General, the early doubts about him were that
he wasn't tough enough; which was true. Marshall on the
outside is a mild, quiet man; his fingers do not go into people's stomachs, yet he proved in those years to be a man of as
much steel and fiber as anyone that administration pro-
duced. He became as close to Robert Kennedy as anyone,
and Kennedy, at the end, probably relied upon his basic
judgment more than that of anyone else. He also had a part
in teaching the young Attorney General that tough talk is
not always toughness; that steel does not necessarily come
from swaggering, boasting and hard talk (the New Frontier
had a lot of that), but from quiet inner conviction. Nonetheless, to the end, the word tough had a fascination for
Robert Kennedy. It was still a quality he admired, though
he might have given a much different description of it by
1968.

The years as Attorney General were very important for
him in a variety of ways. For one thing they gave him an

identifiable public record. Instead of being a shadowy figure slipping in and out of the back door, blamed for all that was bad, and credited with little that was good, he became a man with a record which could be checked. He was more than just an Attorney General, he was like a deputy president, particularly after the Bay of Pigs. He advised the President on almost every major issue, seeing the world from the eye of the storm. (The President quite accurately felt that the traditional advisers who came with the offices were more identified with their own particular agencies than with the Kennedy administration.) He was a good Attorney General, getting better. He made good, even excellent appointments. He gave people their head. Most important, on the great questions of the day, he was very good.

On civil rights both he and his brother entered with a nominal interest, and Robert Kennedy left with a growing sensitivity. They had both come from Massachusetts where the race question was for a long time a minor ethnic political issue. Had they been from Illinois or New York they might have been more immediately sensitive to the complexities and depth of black feelings. Rather they had run in 1960 as traditional liberal Democratic politicians: hold the old coalition together, be *for* (rather than against) the Negro, don't say anything against them, give whoever their anointed leaders are the minimal reward, usually one notch above what the previous administration gave. Besides, 1960 was the last year of the old order. The Negroes, given the 1954 Supreme Court ruling on segregation in the schools, had waited for six years for the courts to give them their share of the action. Now, in 1960, the young restless kids who had received no benefit from the legal change were taking the matter into their own hands. They began with sit-ins, demanding the right to eat bad overpriced hamburgers just like any other American. They radically changed the pace and tempo of the race question in Amer-

ica, and inevitably, the federal government would be involved in a growing number of moral decisions. The Kennedys did not realize this at first, they were still thinking
in traditional terms. They had done a little more for the
Negro than the previous administration and they had not
yet realized that a revolution had started. They were like
most important and influential Americans of that time;
they were far more interested in foreign crises than the
coming domestic storm. In addition, their hesitance to take
the initiative on civil rights at the start of the administration
reflected their nervousness after the narrow victory of 1960;
one sensed that they planned to go slow in the first administration, then run again, in 1964, win by a landslide, and
then move ahead on civil rights.

In 1963 Robert Kennedy decided to meet with a group
of Negro intellectuals and artists. Just why was never clear,
but the impression was strong that he wanted to hear what
was on their minds, wanted to be praised a little, and wanted
to create continuing ties of friendship—perhaps toward
1964. He asked James Baldwin, the peripatetic writer and
protester, to arrange it. Many of the Negroes invited never
exactly understood what it was they were being so impa-
tiently summoned to, but arrived at Baldwin's desperate
plea. The meeting was a disaster. Kennedy totally misjudged
the temper of the Negroes who, meeting in a large group
with a white man, all went to the more militant position.
(Six years later I asked him what he learned from the meeting. He said, "Never meet with more than two or three
Negroes at a time. Never with eighteen. With eighteen it's
hopeless. Everyone has to be more militant. Now I realize
what they were saying, and why, and why they were so
angry, but what was hard to take at the time were the ones
who let me take the roasting and then came over afterward
to sympathize.") A young civil-rights worker who had been
beaten on the head during one of the then-recent Freedom

Rides got up and said that it made him sick being there. He apparently meant that it made him sick having to sit there and ask for his rights which by constitutional right were already his. Kennedy, however, misunderstood and thought him to be saying that it made him sick to be with Robert Kennedy. Kennedy had been under the impression that the Kennedys were *for* the Negroes, and that, of course, the Negroes understood this, and so he pointed to administration accomplishments. They were stunned; to them Kennedy was talking about one drop in a very big bucket, and they had thought he had, at least, realized this, realized how little had been done for the Negroes. At the end of the meeting Baldwin told people that "Bobby Kennedy was a little surprised at the depth of Negro feeling. We were a little shocked at the extent of his naïveté."

But the momentum of American life was headed toward new and militant demands, and the protesters carried the administration with them. Again and again the administration was caught in civil-rights crises, inevitably to land on the side of the Negroes, and inevitably to bring greater affection for the Kennedys from the Negroes. Similarly, there developed in Robert Kennedy a growing sensitivity to the problem of black and white in America. The Kennedys became committed on civil rights in those years simply because there was nowhere else to go, except backward. Thus in 1968, in a black neighborhood, a handmade sign over a Kennedy storefront would read:

> *Kennedy white but alright.*
> *The one before, he opened the door.*

On foreign affairs he became a surprisingly cool and thoughtful influence. In an administration heavy with political scientists, Robert Kennedy's basic value to the President was that he had excellent common sense, judged people well, and often followed his own best instincts. (Following one's best instincts and common sense would have avoided both the Bay of Pigs and the ground war in Vietnam.) His role grew after the Bay of Pigs. The President needed him, and one sensed that the President set out to expand Robert's world, picking the Attorney General for foreign assignment as the President's representative and thus putting his younger brother into situations which might expand and broaden his view of the world. I went on his first major trip, in August 1961, when Kennedy represented the President at the independence ceremonies at the Ivory Coast. He was shy, uncertain of himself. (I remember him wrestling with both his French and his speech: "Your President, Houphouet-Boigny, is the George Washington of your country." Then he listed all the similarities between American and Ivorien history.) But even here, certain characteristics came through. He wanted a candid and thorough briefing before leaving and he was appalled by the lack of knowledge and interest of the first three men the State Department sent over. He kept sending them back until the Department sent over a young man named Brandon Grove who had just spent three years in the Ivory Coast, and who knew the background and the current political balance. Kennedy immediately drafted him for the trip, and later took him on his world tour in 1962. The other thing he demonstrated on arrival was his disdain for normal diplomatic procedures, many of which are hopelessly out of date in a contemporary world. The embassy there had scheduled a series of meetings with all the official people. Instead, he wanted to talk with students, labor leaders (as much as they had them), and of course he wanted to get out into the boondocks to see how the people lived. The embassy felt he ran roughshod over it, pushed its members around, made unnecessary and unfair demands, and insulted its good Ivorien friends. Almost everyone else loved it. This would not be the last embassy to feel this way.

He behaved particularly well during the Cuban missile-crisis in 1962. At the height of the crisis, when the two main choices were a naval blockade and a surprise air strike to eliminate the missile sites, most advisers appeared to favor the bombing. Robert Kennedy strongly opposed it. The air strike, he said, sounded like a Pearl Harbor in reverse. It would be hard to explain to the rest of the world—particularly after the Bay of Pigs—why a great nation was bombing such a small one, and most people would doubt that the missile sites really existed. He did not want his brother to become the Tojo of the sixties. Dean Acheson, a power man and a man with a considerable reputation, attempted to destroy the Attorney General's argument. The young man, he said, simply wasn't dealing with the realities of power and this was a situation where you used power. But Kennedy insisted: American tradition and ideals were completely against such a bombing raid and the world would never understand it. Douglas Dillon, originally for the air strikes, swung around on the basis of the Attorney General's argument. "What changed my mind," he later told Elie Abel, who chronicled the crisis, "was Bob's argument that we ought to be true to ourselves as Americans, that surprise attack was not in our tradition. Frankly these considerations had not occurred to me until Bob raised them. . . ." Later during the same crisis the Attorney General was useful again. Khrushchev had sent a Friday note which was conciliatory but then made a Saturday broadcast which seemed more threatening. It was Robert Kennedy's simple but sound idea to ignore the Saturday message and simply respond to the Friday one.

On Vietnam he was one of the principal authors of the counterinsurgency commitment. An early enthusiast, he forced everyone in Washington to go to special classes on counterinsurgency. Yet even then his judgment was helpful. During 1963 when I was in Vietnam and was not exactly the favorite reporter of the Kennedy administration, the administration saw that a major foreign-policy disaster was shaping up and wished that the crisis would go away or, failing that, that my colleagues and I would go away. Michael Forrestal, the White House man on Vietnam, saw, probably more than any other Washington official, what was coming. He saw it clearly and used his influence to change Washington policy. At the time he told me that if you wanted to get dissident ideas through to the President (which is a very important thing, given the constantly increasing power of the executive branch, the natural isolation of the Presidency, and the instinct of most men to tell powerful men what they want to hear), the single person most open to suggestion and to accepting bad news was Robert Kennedy.

Those were nevertheless good and heady days for the Kennedys, a confluence of power, intelligence, style and glamour perhaps never seen before in this country. Everyone, it seemed, was bright, handsome and tough and had a good-looking wife. They set a style which those of us on the outside might envy, for it was true that the Kennedys, with their wealth, could have free what money could not buy. They could get other immensely talented people to work for them who would not work for other politicians no matter how correct the politician's ideological position or voting record. Those who were simply wealthy found glamour; those who had glamour and wealth found power. It was, in fact, too good a time. They inhaled people; thoughtful journalists and intellectuals who could not be bought in the real sense were taken over by the Kennedys and the glamour. They became too close, they went regularly to Hickory Hill, saw only what they wanted to see, and finally in the eyes of their colleagues they became Kennedy satellites, Kennedy insiders. Their gossip would be listened to, their presence at a dinner party sought, their post-administration books bought, but finally they would be seen as Kennedy men, and this would come back to haunt Robert Kennedy. Years later, when his own candidacy was advanced, many of the people who now spoke for him were a little tarnished, their independence questioned, their intellectual judgment no longer so valued. There was, in some places, a Camelot backlash. Robert Kennedy would be in a position where his enemies would be armed and his supporters disarmed. Other younger men coming along, viewing his candidacy, would deliberately stand a little further back: no one was going to inhale them. He was not going to get the benefit of the doubt.

It would always be a point of dispute: whether the dominant force was Kennedyism, the Kennedys first, right or wrong, or whether it was issues, those particular causes he came to articulate, which formed the real pull. To some journalists and critics resisting the pull and the glamour, there was a feeling that the Kennedys, starting back before 1960, had always practiced manipulation with issues; that the basic inner ideology was simply The Family, right or wrong; and that many in the inner circle were motivated not so much by causes and social issues, as simply by the fact that this team was a winning one—it had won once before and now there would be a restoration. Thus there was a feeling among many reporters, particularly in the early and mid-sixties, that it was not enough to like the Kennedys part way, to be partially sympathetic but still to write about their warts (though they had fewer warts). One had to go all the way with them. (Laura Bergquist of *Look*, a sympathetic journalist-friend of the family, recalled asking the then Attorney General a tough question about bombings in the South at a magazine writer's luncheon. Kennedy, unhappy with the subject, fumbled the question. Later an angry Ethel Kennedy grabbed Miss Bergquist in the ladies' room and said to her fiercely, "I thought you were a friend of my husband's.") This all led to a feeling that the Kennedys were overzealously policing up their image, and finally a belief that the Manchester affair, messy and demeaning as it was, was exactly what they had long deserved. (Even though Manchester did violate his contract, and Robert Kennedy, caught between his sister-in-law and his own political career, behaved honorably, if perhaps unwisely from a political point of view.)

My own feeling was that this sense of Kennedyism had begun to ebb in the last two years of Robert Kennedy's life; that it was one more reflection of the change in his viewpoint; that in the post-assassination period, issues and human grievances began to consume him and that he judged people not so much on how they related to the Kennedys, but on how they related to issues. Hence some of the differences between the old Kennedy advisers and journalistic friends, and the newer more issue-oriented Kennedy friends and journalistic friends: George Smathers, the Florida Senator who led the fight against minimum wage for migrant workers was an old Kennedy friend; Cesar Chavez was a new Kennedy friend.

But the symbol of the conflict between the Kennedys and their critics was the uneasy relationship between the candidate and *The New York Times*. Kennedy got on reasonably well with the reporters, but the editors were another thing; there was a tension going back to the early Jack Kennedy days when John Oakes, the editor of the editorial page, had once implied that Sorensen, not Jack Kennedy, was primarily responsible for the writing of *Profiles in Courage.* Jack Kennedy went to considerable length to point out that this was false. That tension had never eased. The great strength of *The Times* is that it will stand alone; it can and does resist fad, idol, and even president of the United States. Hence an almost inevitable clash between two powerful contemporary institutions—*The New York Times* and the Kennedys. The Kennedys, because they were liberals, assumed *The Times* would be in their hip pocket, or at least sympathetic, which it clearly was not. It was as if this very assumption of the Kennedys brought out a stronger sense of *The Times'* independence, a conscious desire not to be swept away. (Thus Kennedy would be annoyed with what he felt was *The Times'* instinct for publishing photographs of the handsome young Mayor of New York, John Lindsay, playing tennis or riding a bike, rather than of the handsome young Senator from New York. He once asked Mankiewicz to call *The Times* to suggest that the paper photograph Kennedy playing handball in the Senate gym. Mankiewicz did. *The Times* was not amused.) *The Times* editors, for their part, felt the Kennedys were manipulative on issues and manipulative of the press. I remember being with the young publisher of *The Times.* Arthur Ochs Sulzberger, in early 1966 when his wife criticized him sharply for the abundance of Bobby stories in his paper; she insisted that he was going to be responsible for making Kennedy president. At the end, during his last campaign, there seemed finally to be a certain justification to the Kennedy complaints that there was a double standard against them, that *The Times* was viewing Robert Kennedy more on the past than on the present, and lent credence to the old attacks on Kennedy for ruthlessness and spending too much money. (The

Oregon campaign, *The Times* wrote, was "too relentless and too aggressive in its single-minded pursuit of power.") There was some bitterness later in the year when Nelson Rocke-feller, running belatedly for the Republican nomination, began spending money, in the words of one Kennedy aide, "like a drunken sailor"—with the enthusiastic support of *The Times*.

That time of excitement ended with the assassination. In those post-assassination days, Robert Kennedy was like a man in shock. He had devoted everything to his older brother, had thought little of himself, and now it was all gone, insanely destroyed. He was also without a political base, for Lyndon Johnson was now President and Robert Kennedy and Johnson had always been opponents. The sharp things Johnson had said about Jack in 1960 rolled off Jack's back, but not off Robert's; and Robert Kennedy had reciprocated by ignoring Johnson during the years in office. There was deep hostility and suspicion. Robert Kennedy offered himself as ambassador to South Vietnam and was rejected by the President who thought it too dangerous. He wanted the vice-presidency. Some of his advisers, like Kenny O'Donnell, suggested a frontal attack—putting so much pressure on through the party organization, which was at that time still more pro-Kennedy than pro-Johnson, that the President would have to yield. But he turned this down and started to campaign.

He went to Poland where he was greeted by tumultuous crowds. He broke all kinds of protocol and enraged the American Embassy by disregarding its instructions, showing up late for official dinners, barnstorming all over the country. At one point, standing on top of a car, he began to speak to a group crowding around. Inside the car was the patrician ambassador John Moors Cabot who told a Kennedy aide, "Would you mind telling the Attorney General the roof is falling in on us." This delighted the aides; they took the words and inscribed them on a silver tray which they gave to the Attorney General. Polish officials were furious with his conduct. "Do you know who you shook hands with this morning in the market?" asked an indignant deputy minister of foreign affairs. "My maid." The trip seemed to rejuvenate him.

But Lyndon Johnson was unmoved. He did not want Robert Kennedy as his vice-president. Kennedy of course knew this would happen, that he would be the last person Johnson wanted ". . . because my name is Kennedy, because he wants a Johnson administration with no Kennedys in it, because we travel different paths, because I suppose some businessmen would object and I'd cost them a few votes in the South." Eventually the President called Kennedy in to break the news. It was a relatively pleasant meeting, Johnson praised Kennedy's past service, said he had a bright future, wanted him to run the campaign, but did not want him on the ticket. As the Attorney General left he turned and said almost wistfully, "I could have helped you a lot." But it did not end well; a few days later Johnson called in three reporters and over a very long lunch regaled them with the story of how he had broken the news to Kennedy. He told how Kennedy had gulped when he heard it. Kennedy was furious when he learned of this; the already bad feelings between the two became even worse. At the convention Johnson was still nervous about his own hold on the party, and the Kennedy electricity. A film on John F. Kennedy had been carefully censored and just as carefully scheduled by the President. There was no mention of Robert Kennedy in it, and it was not shown until after the vice-presidential nomination was completed. Robert Kennedy introduced the film and it was the most dramatic and emotional moment of the entire convention, fifteen minutes of wild cheering. Finally he spoke, quoting from *Romeo and Juliet:*

When he shall die
Take him and cut him out in little stars,
And he will make the face of heaven so fine
That all the world will be in love with night
And pay no worship to the garish sun.

Without a base, anxious to keep his career alive and continue the restoration ("And if anything happens to me Bobby will take my place, and if anything happens to him it will be Teddy," Jack Kennedy had once said describing how he had taken Joe Jr.'s place as the family politician), Robert Kennedy turned to New York for the Senate seat. It was not something which appealed to him; there was already one Kennedy in the Senate, and besides Robert Kennedy was an activist, a doer, he did not particularly want to be a junior member of a deliberative body. But there was nowhere else to go, and he came to New York to run against Kenneth Keating. To a degree this would undermine even more his credentials with liberals, for Keating was a man who, though leading the league in anti-Communist, anti-Nasser and anti-Sukarno speeches, had an enviable record for domestic legislation. Many liberals would finally vote for Kennedy, but they would do it grudgingly, feeling somehow that they were deserting Keating who had a right to their loyalty. It was a fairly banal campaign. Each ran around the state courting the ethnic vote, particularly the Jewish vote which was regarded as a swing factor. They made every temple breakfast in town; they wore their yarmulkes all over the city. Keating recounted his many speeches against Nasser and said he would make Israel a member of NATO; Kennedy imported Abe Ribicoff to talk to Jews. "The things you are saying against Bob Kennedy are exactly the same things you said four years ago against Jack Kennedy," Ribicoff told Jewish groups.

The main issue against Kennedy was that he was a carpetbagger; that plus the fact that no one was angry with

Keating. He was white-haired, he was nice, he looked like
a Senator and he was virtuous on the Goldwater issue (his
virtue consisted of failing to endorse Goldwater; an endorse-
ment, of course, would have been suicidal). He was not,
however, a particularly good target for a young man, a
carpetbagger, and a man around whom a good deal of suspicion still swirled. Yet Kennedy was the heir of the great
family, and a nation still mourned an assassinated President. "I am for Robert Kennedy," wrote Murray Kempton
who reflected some of the emotion of the times but was to
become a bitter critic in 1968, "because he is a decent and
talented young man terribly wounded whom I do not want
to look upon wounded further. This is like being for Bonnie
Prince Charlie; it has to do with commitment to a divine
right and there are no reasonable arguments for a divine
right." Two things finally sealed Kennedy's victory. One
was his use of television which was far better than Keating's. Kennedy's television spots were fresh and modern;
Keating always seemed to be backed by an American flag.
The Kennedy radio spots were well done too. Over and over
the voice would come: "Think about it for a minute: which
of the candidates running for United States Senator has the
better chance of becoming a great U.S. Senator . . . a *great*
U.S. Senator. . . . On November 3, vote for Robert Kennedy."
It was effective, slick stuff; it caught just the right implica-
tion for the Kennedy camp, that though Keating was a very
nice old man, perhaps he was not really as good as his
voting record, maybe he wasn't a really strong figure. The
other asset was Goldwater. In New York State Goldwater
was the kiss of death. Johnson would carry New York by
2.6 million votes. Kennedy was aware of this as the campaign progressed. He put greater emphasis on supporting
not just Bob Kennedy, but the Johnson-Humphrey-Kennedy
ticket; he emphasized that he was the only candidate who

was *for* Lyndon Johnson. In the final days Hubert Humphrey came in to campaign for him. Thus he won, but with the galling fact that he had come in on Lyndon Johnson's coattails. It annoyed him. The rest of the country might not pay attention to it, but it was something that he and Lyndon Johnson both knew, and that was two people too many.

Nominally a Senate seat from New York is a weak power base. The Senate bestows power by seniority and by security so that the most important and powerful members come from small states with one-party electorates and one-crop economies. They were the men who survived, who worked their way up in the Washington jungle. They would return home briefly to make the pro-sheep farmer speech and then return to Washington where they gained seniority; they played the game and eventually dominated the Washington scene. This was the direct opposite of Kennedy politics, the provocative politics of youth and energy, injecting themselves into issues, speaking out, having immediate media impact on the world outside Washington rather than the world inside. The Kennedys are not known for waiting.

Under normal conditions a junior senate seat, particularly from New York where one must speak for the polyglot of ethnic, business, industrial and labor groups, might have led him to quick obscurity, especially with his party in the White House, or might have saddled him with endless speeches promoting all of New York's vast and conflicting groups. The Ukrainian speech one day, the Jewish speech the next, then the pro-cop speech and then the pro-parking violator speech. But the Johnson presidency soon became dominated by Vietnam, and the Democratic party became at once the party of power and the party of dissent. Kennedy was thus pushed more and more into a special role; because he was a Kennedy, his constituency was not just

New York, his constituency was national. On issue after
issue, as Johnson became imprisoned by the war, people
looked to Kennedy for leadership. Gradually, through the
hearings he held on urban problems in the Senate, through
trips to Mississippi and to the grape pickers in California
and to the Indians in New Mexico, he became the spokesman for the poor and the restless and the dissatisfied in
America. Thus when America suddenly began to go through
great social change, all of this heightened by the war in
Vietnam (which drained off money and sharpened existing
divisions), Kennedy was, by chance and not especially desire, on the outside looking in. He was outside the power
establishment and he could feel, himself, some of the futil-
ity which the dispossessed felt. His course became one of
increased radicalism. "The difference between him and
Humphrey," said one of his friends midway through the
campaign, "is that Humphrey started out, in 1948, outside
the establishment and slowly and steadily was incorporated
into it, step by step until, in 1968, he was an official establishment figure. When the columnists talk about Humphrey
being the man of reconciliation because he can bring together the labor unions and the Southern governors, they're
really talking about him reconciling two different parts of
the establishment—they may have made it by quite different
roads, but they're both there nevertheless. Now Kennedy
began in power, but because of events was thrown out of
the establishment and thus has looked at American society
from the outside. There is one other difference; one was out
in 1948 and the other was out in 1967, and that means a
very great deal of difference in outlook."

IV ━━━━━━━━━━━━━

Nebraska came and went quickly. It was a triumph of imported organization and style. Indiana had taken all the time and effort, but the Kennedys, it was one of their great assets, had the resources to send yet another team into Nebraska to schedule the candidate properly, to save his time, and to get him the proper exposure. McCarthy was already stretched too thin in Indiana. His eye was on Oregon and California. He lacked sufficient organizational structure; he had virtually forgotten about Nebraska until too late. Then his campaign was a disaster; a hodgepodge of misscheduling, wasted time and effort, and long hours trying to get to the wrong town. His frustration built as he sensed that the Kennedys were moving around smoothly, seeing more people, getting in and out of towns quickly, and choosing the right towns. There is occasionally a moment when a candidate finds himself *lost* in an area, and that happened to McCarthy in Nebraska. Nebraska is a difficult state for a Democrat to campaign in anyway; its population is stretched thin and far. At the outset the Kennedys had been more worried about Nebraska than any other state. It had treated John Kennedy roughly, and it seemed to distrust Easterners; Easterners were different and had too long imposed their ideas, their taste, their accents, and worse, their government on the Midwest. In particular, the Kennedys, Eastern, rich and patrician, had seemed out of place in Nebraska. Jack Kennedy had hated the idea of farm issues. He had once appointed John Kenneth Galbraith, a former agricultural economist, his chief farm expert, saying, "Ken, I don't want to hear about farm policy from anyone but you—and I don't want to hear about it from you either." Orville Freeman, named Secretary of Agriculture under Kennedy, had explained his appointment at the time: "I think it has something to do with the fact that they don't have a school of agriculture at Harvard." Now Robert Kennedy would mock that cultural gap between east and west in town after town in Nebraska: "Don't you just feel it when you're looking at a fellow farmer? I come from New York, a great farming state," he would say, laughing at their skeptical looks. "What? You don't accept that? Well we're first in the production of sour cherries. . . ."

The scheduling had been good. They had been aided by Phil Sorensen, Ted's brother and a former lieutenant governor, and they managed to hit all the towns larger than 10,000. The Kennedys rented a train and used it to tie together many of the otherwise isolated towns—towns which had been formed in the first place because of their proximity to the Union Pacific. The Kennedys had reinvented trains as a means of campaigning in Indiana. Trains now had made the complete cycle in American politics, from the only means of transportation to gimmick transportation scheduled by a candidate to give the television crews something extra to cover; remembrances of an America Past. And it had worked. When Robert Kennedy had boarded the Wabash Cannonball he had no less a fellow traveler than David Brinkley himself, there to cover Americana for NBC. That particular ride had gone very well. Indeed when the Kennedy canvassers checked with the public about which of the candidate's television commercials they liked the best, a majority cited the one about the Wabash Cannonball. This irritated Goodwin and the advertising people a good deal, and delighted Mankiewicz and the press staff. The train was cheap, colorful, and easy on the candidate. "We never realized how easy those old-style politicians had it," Dutton said one day after a train ride. "The trains are very easy. The candidate gets on, and he can rest. He has a whole car in which he can work with his advisers. There's no bumping around in the clouds, no jumping on and off the plane, no fighting your way through crowd after crowd. The crowds assemble for you; if there's any shoving, it's not you who gets shoved. You talk for a few minutes, you quote George Bernard Shaw so you don't leave any reporters behind, and then you can rest again."

In Nebraska the train touched tiny towns which had not seen an American presidential candidate since William Jennings Bryan. It was a tour which a lesser candidate, or a less well-known celebrity, might not have been able to make. Had McCarthy made the trip, the crowds simply might not have come. But this was a Kennedy and for days before there had been signs saying, "Yes, Robert Kennedy Is Coming to Ogallala," or "Meet Robert Kennedy Saturday in Downtown North Platte." Aboard the train the national reporters could hear the incredibly excited voices of the local radio reporters: "It's due any minute now, due in a minute. . . . Yes, there it is ladies and gentlemen, I see the light, I see the light of the train, it's coming down Main Street, people are running toward it, the train is *slowing down.* The children are pushing toward it. The police are fighting to keep the crowd back. Now the train is stopping. I see the press getting off. . . . *Television* crews are getting off. The crowd is surging forward, and *Yes,* Robert *Kennedy* is coming back on the platform. He's waving to the crowd. He looks smaller than you expect. . . ." He was in a good mood aboard the train. Earlier the train had gone through Julesburg, Colorado, the birthplace of Fred Dutton (a fact discovered at the last minute), and Ethel Kennedy, not telling anyone, had spent several hours making up posters. When the train stopped, she and friends rushed out and started a Dutton demonstration. "Sock it to 'em Freddy," "Fred Dutton's Brother for Attorney General," "Make Fred, Not War," read the signs. They demanded a speech and the candidate, now joining in, shouted: "Tell us about George Bernard Shaw, Fred."

The crowds were good all along the way. The candidate was relaxed, telling the crowds: "Richard Nixon is speaking up in front of the train. We thought that was only fair. He has no crowd at all." Then he would talk low key, a fairly conservative pitch: that the local people knew more about their business than some bureaucrat in Washington (which went over well; even in Washington no one loves faceless Washington bureaucrats), and a little bit on law and order and the divisions in the country, and then fairly hard on the war. Frank Morrison, the former governor and one of the few Democrats with real statewide appeal, had noted that the war was very simply *the* issue in Nebraska, the gut issue. People wouldn't talk about it much, he said, because they think it's unpatriotic to talk a lot about it, but it's there. The farmers were angry too, restless in a time of rising costs and low prices, and aware that most of the other whites in America had never had it so good. They were restless and angry and Kennedy told them they were being cheated, that he favored collective bargaining for them, a popular stand.

But there were still problems, and in some ways the campaign was not jelling the way they had hoped. The crowds were still coming, that part of the magic still worked, but the politicians were not. The bosses, and the leaders of the

Democratic party apparatus, were still suspicious and unreceptive, and this was being demonstrated by a marked
migration to Hubert Humphrey. It was becoming clearer
and clearer that Robert Kennedy's problem with the machines was very deep and serious, and that the apparatus
was almost as hostile to him as it was to McCarthy. For the
first time in many years, the party machinery, which had
traditionally been reasonably sympathetic to the pressures
and whims of the party eggheads and liberals, was un-
responsive to two candidates representing the intellectual
element.

The relationship between the Kennedys and the party
machinery had always been a tenuous one; they were not
of it, and yet they had never fought it, even in their earlier
years. In Massachusetts, where local politics are particularly
venal, they had simply by-passed the apparatus. They had
developed their own breathtaking popularity and that meant
that the party machinery would not make a frontal challenge. They were able to control the state delegation at
conventions, but in return they never really used any of
their power, popularity, or resources to clean up Massachusetts politics. Reformers in Massachusetts tend to be
somewhat cooler to the Kennedys than reformers in other
states; they have seen more of their cool indifferent side.
Massachusetts was a quagmire which the Kennedys tol-
erated and were careful not to step into. In 1960 their relationship with the machinery was guarded, but improved
steadily. Mayor Daley of Chicago, the most important and
most sophisticated of the traditional politicians, had been
for Jack Kennedy, first because of his friendship with Joe
Kennedy but also, and equally important, because he sensed
a winner. "Daley has sense enough to go with classy politicians, even if they're men he doesn't feel at ease with,"
said one student of machines. "That makes him different

from most machine people who shun anyone they don't feel at ease with." But with Bobby Kennedy it was a little different. They sensed in him a puritan; he was not above prosecuting dishonest local *Democratic* officials and in that sense, he was as dangerous as a Republican. (In Illinois, the Cook County machine cares more about who wins county attorney races than who wins the U.S. Senate race. The power of investigation is a very important negative power.)

In New York he had seemed to side increasingly, though sometimes ineffectually, with the reformers in their regular fights with the organization. He preferred to be photographed with the reformers and work in private with the apparatus people. In 1964, meeting with the varying bosses of New York State before deciding to run for the Senate, a photographer happened by the hotel suite and took a number of pictures. He was asked to throw them away. The machine people sensed that in future conflicts *this* Kennedy would side more and more with their enemies, and they did not like his style and his direction. The machines were dependent upon the old-style control of poor Negro areas. As it was, their own black leaders there (Toms) were being jeopardized by the new angry militants whom the poverty programs were supposed to help, and with whom Kennedy was so publicly identified. The apparatus people sensed that if Kennedy were elected, it would speed them that much more quickly to obsolescence. He was only forty-two and his people were often younger; they were all in their fifties and sixties.

(When Frank O'Connor was going to run against Rockefeller in New York, the Kennedys had opposed him. He was the best of the old breed, they noted, and they wanted the best of the new breed. If the young reformers did not understand what they meant, the worst of the old breed certainly did.) Kennedy was just very different, and he identified himself with all the new and threatening trends, even long hair. A story put out by Dick Daley's people tells of Kennedy's having gone, in 1967—when he was considering the race—to see the Mayor. He had said, my father is not well, and my brother is dead, and I now regard you as an old friend of the family. May I turn to you for advice? The Mayor said yes, that was fine. So Kennedy asked for advice, and Daley gave him some: "Get your hair cut." The story is perhaps apocryphal, but symbolic nevertheless. If the existing officials of the Democratic party lack a powerful sense of social change, they do have a sense of survival. Robert Kennedy, like Gene McCarthy, threatened that survival. Hubert Humphrey did not.

This had been a year of great surprises, though many of them highly predictable, and perhaps the greatest surprise was the resurrection of Hubert Humphrey. One was surprised by how easily it was done, and how readily the party faithful moved toward a man who had never proven himself in any sort of national election; a man who was closely tied to a deeply unpopular administration, and who was avoiding any primary fights, indeed a man who stood a very good chance of winning a nomination but losing an election (normally a patented Republican strategy). In early 1968 no one had seemed a frailer politician than Humphrey. Had one wanted to do a study of what the war in Vietnam had done to a generation of older American liberals, Humphrey would have been exhibit A. The war was destroying him with his liberal constituency, and as the war progressed, or failed to progress, his own style seemed increasingly out of date. He was a politician of the old school; hot and heavy oratory, never understate when you can overstate, party loyalty above all else (his Democratic arm around the Democratic arm of Lester Maddox)—they were all required qualities in the old politics, but dubious assets in this age. Even the old-style colleagues of Humphrey were now disappearing; Paul Douglas and Mennen Williams were out, Nelson Rockefeller, George Romney and Chuck Percy were in. (Romney and Percy were milestones in American politics. We had formerly trusted sons of very wealthy families in politics so long as they were not con-servative—inherited wealth is intolerable in a conservative, for the rich do not need to steal. But now we had gone to trusting businessmen, even self-made businessmen, so long as they didn't look like businessmen.) Humphrey was markedly, relentlessly, of the old school.

In the age of cool he was out; in a time of understate-ment he overstated; in a time when television made brief speeches mandatory, he still spoke with the cadence and length of a radio orator. At a time when the intellectual theorists of his own party were increasingly dubious and pessimistic about the course of American life, Humphrey was incorrigibly ebullient, talking of the politics of joy and happiness. The more he talked, the more it grated. (In-tellectuals consider optimism permissible if the times are clearly bad and frightening to an entire nation, i.e., a de-pression or a world war. Then the optimist who can inject new hope is desirable. But when the challenge seems hidden to much of the nation, as it did in 1968, optimism is unfashionable. The intellectuals demand someone who can convey to the rest of the nation that this is a dark time, and then hold up a glimmer of hope. Humphrey's optimism had been born during the New Deal days and both it and his style of projecting it had never changed. However, the country had changed a great deal.) Was the new style that of underplaying idealism? Humphrey shouted out. His ear was desperately bad and out of tune. He went on television and talked about himself in the third person, and it sounded like a relic of Fourth of July bombast. There was a quality of true sadness in all this; the liberals had loved Hubert back in the fifties. He was proof that liberalism did not necessarily exist only in the dark alien cities of the nation, but that it could flourish and win in the good clean air of the Midwest. They had not minded his good Midwestern enthusiasms and excesses, for they had been liberal excesses and enthusiasms. But now these excesses had been turned to a dubious cause; he had spoken in Saigon to American State Department officers about their *wonderful* mission there, God save the piaster, and now it was all ending badly because of the war. Joe Rauh of the ADA, an old friend of Humphrey's, would listen to all Humphrey's defenses of the war, and would nod and say yes, Hubert, yes. But don't you realize what everyone else in America realizes—that if you weren't vice-president you would be leading the dissent on it. Indeed a meeting had been arranged in December between Humphrey and the leaders of the ADA. Once his close friends, they were now his pickets. Feeling had run so high before he arrived that Arthur Schlesinger took the liberals aside and said, Look, I know we feel strongly, but he's a good man and he is the vice-president and our old friend. We've got to be polite and show restraint. Everyone agreed. Then Humphrey arrived and immediately began by saying that he had just talked with Adam Malik of Indonesia, and Malik had said that it was the U.S. intervention in Vietnam which had saved the Indonesian domino, and Schlesinger had interrupted: "Oh bullshit Hubert!"

Humphrey at the start of the year had been a badly crippled politician, a symbol of Lyndon Johnson's ability to take much and give little. (The Reverend Jesse Jackson, one of Martin Luther King's militant leaders in the North, would say in sadness of Humphrey, "Hubert Humphrey is a grape of hope that has been turned into a raisin of despair by the sunshine of Lyndon Johnson.") There was a touch of the clown in the tone with which Humphrey talked about the President. He could go on television and say: "I think I know who are men of peace, and the man of peace that I see in this country—but peace with justice and peace with freedom—is President Lyndon Johnson." It was one of the final victories of Lyndon Johnson that he had made Hubert Humphrey sound like Richard Nixon. But then suddenly Lyndon Johnson had withdrawn from the race and Humphrey had been reborn. Now all those great resources of the presidency which Lyndon Johnson had been unable to use for himself because of the war, could be used for Hubert Humphrey. He suddenly had the advantages of the presidency without the disadvantages. He could barely believe it. He had been out of the country when Johnson had withdrawn and when he came back the first question he asked his staff was whether Bobby had a lock on it. Kennedy did not, and day after day it was Kennedy who was further from the lock and Humphrey who was closer to it. For a moment the war had simply evaporated, the issue had disappeared. To an older generation of liberals he was the good Hubert again, the old Hubert. (It was a generational thing; among important younger members of the party his support was noticeably weaker. The only important young man on his way up who was backing Humphrey was Adlai Stevenson III—a tie bound in part out of family loyalty to his father, and also in part out of family dislike or uneasiness with the Kennedys.) It was back to 1948, all of this had never happened.

Humphrey suddenly started getting a very good press, particularly out of Washington. Washington is a company town and Humphrey was the good company liberal; indeed he was the only company-certified candidate in either race. Humphrey had been gathering due bills in Washington for as long as he had been gathering them among the party workers, and now he was calling them in. For the last year or two he had managed to give the impression to those in Washington, in the inner circle, that he was loyal, but agonized and loyal. He might, knowing that a certain influential columnist was also agonized and loyal, stop by for breakfast with him where they would share their agony, and Humphrey's confidence would be protected. But his deeper darker side would be properly viewed so that the right men in Washington knew how agonized Humphrey was, even if the rest of the country did not. Now running, he got sympathetic columns from those liberals who liked the war: Hubert really believes in the war, and understands it, and from those liberal columnists who did not: Hubert doesn't believe in the war, but has been imprisoned by Johnson, just wait til he's on his own. Indeed if many of the senior Washington commentators were upset by the war, they seemed even more upset by what McCarthy and Kennedy were doing with it. Perhaps it would all end badly, for the Paris peace talks were a dubious proposition under Lyndon Johnson: one did not hire the architect to tear down his own prize building. Perhaps if they dragged on, the old war would reappear and the new Hubert instead of the old would be unveiled at Chicago. But for the moment the Kennedy people were angry; they recognized all the good and hard work Humphrey had done in the party vineyard, but they were bitter about the good press he was getting in liberal quarters (particularly *The New York Times* editorial page; if one were a former *Times* reporter one heard about that regularly). They felt that this was giving a respectability to an old outdated system which was trying to protect itself; an alliance of Southern Democrats, big city machines and big labor. An alliance which annoyed the Kennedys primarily because it existed, and secondly because it wasn't going for them.

But Humphrey the party man was reaping the party reward. He was like Richard Nixon in more than just speech, perhaps speech was an outgrowth of association and habit. He had been the good party loyalist, speaking at every dinner, eating all those cold green peas, praising all those overweight sheriffs, shaking hands with all those aldermen, remembering their wives' names, showing up in Kansas in the cold winter when the plane connections were terrible and he had a cold, appearing at dinky fund raisings; always ebullient and finding *virtue* in every Democrat there. If there was any doubt in 1968 about how well Humphrey had served the country (and there was a great deal of it), there was no doubt at all about how well he had served the party. And, of course, many of the faithful understood the party better than the nation; a good many of them failed to make any distinction at all.

For the party faithful Hubert was sound and safe and loyal, and loyalty was the most important. The structure of the party is not based on imagination or creativity or social conscience, it is based on loyalty (the honest politician, the joke goes, is the one who, when bought, stays bought). It is based on working your way up one notch, not threatening the man above you, for you might be threatened from below. Thus while Kennedy was out working the primaries, Humphrey and his people were very quietly going around and picking up the delegates, cashing in the due bills. Kennedy, campaigning on the road, was in serious trouble. His delegate counts were not good, the delegates were pro-Humphrey though Humphrey's hold was a very tenuous one. Part of the problem was that as Kennedy plunged more into the campaign and saw more and more of America, of the dispossessed and the under-privileged, the more he was moved by it and the more he identified with it. Accordingly, he identified less and less with the party apparatus and the professionals. He now began to see them as the kind of people who were responsible for the existing system, who were indeed blocking the needed changes, and he was not at ease with them. If they saw him as a threat, they were right, because he saw them as a stumbling block. In city after city he would meet with them. He was not good at the small talk, not good at the little jokes which were a staple of the profession; he could not do the little social things easily, press the flesh. Their stock in trade was small talk and his was not, and when they left they often thought him a cold one indeed.

During the campaign a curious phenomenon developed. At night when there might have been time to go to dinner with a delegate, or a politician or two, he rarely did. He went out with a few friends, occasionally an assistant, often journalist friends—not because they might write something nice about him, though that helped—but because he seemed almost bored by politics and wanted to talk about something else. One of his great favorites was Jack Newfield, a young radical writer for *The Village Voice*. Once, invited to Hickory Hill for a great party where all the old friends—Katzenbach, General Taylor, MacNamara—were also socializing, Newfield had balked: "You don't expect me to go in there and drink and talk with all those war criminals do you?" Kennedy would still meet with delegates and they would talk, but he would withdraw from them; and they sensed this.

All of this became clear one night in Omaha when Kennedy went before a Jefferson-Jackson Day dinner. It was a Friday, and Kennedy had enjoyed an excellent day; he had visited a dozen towns between Lincoln and Omaha, and his crowds had been good and his receptions warm. He had seemed to get stronger as the day went on, enjoying himself, relaxed. Then came the dinner. It was awkward to start with because Humphrey was to be the main speaker, and thus Kennedy seemed an interloper. Kennedy was to speak first and then leave. When he first walked into the hall (journalistic applausemeter: Kennedy polite applause; Humphrey warm applause), he already looked different, tense, his hands knotted. The band played the national anthem, the soloist sang, Bobby sang, and no one else sang. It was the kind of thing he loved. His speech was to be brief, but the prepared text was a good one. It was short, sharp, one of his best: "Too much and for too long we have confused our achievements with wealth, and measured our greatness with the statistics of the Gross National Product. But the Gross National Product counts air pollution and cigarette advertising and ambulances to clear our highways of carnage. It counts Whitman's rifle and Speck's knife and television programs that glorify violence—the better to sell goods to our children." Yet when he spoke he was terrible. He rushed through the speech, lost the balance and the cadence of it, dropped his lines, garbled his thoughts. He seemed in a hurry to leave; indeed the moment he finished he did.

Later, talking with a reporter about it, he was highly critical of his own performance. He had not turned them on, he said, and he had really blown the whole thing. A cold evening. Just cold. Then he added: "They're just not my kind of crowd." It was a curious thing for a candidate to say about other politicians.

A brief respite in Nebraska. His mother, campaigning on the west coast, had replied to criticism of Kennedy wealth by saying, "it's our money and we're free to spend it any way we please." Teddy Kennedy, asked about this quote, had partially saved the day by saying, "That's why we didn't make mother finance chairman." Now the candidate was being asked by a wire-service reporter about the quotes. He read Rose Kennedy's remarks and Teddy's reply and paled noticeably. No comment, he said. Not even an off-the-record comment? asked the reporter. Okay, said the candidate, "That's why we *did* make her finance chairman."

The day of the debacle with the Omaha party officials, he was relaxed again. It was a warm sunny day in the suburban areas of Omaha and the crowds were bigger than expected, more receptive. He spoke well and answered questions at length, in no rush to go anywhere on this lovely day. Was he worried about the population explosion? "I think every individual should work out his own arrangement. I've worked out my own arrangement, but obviously it won't work for everybody else." Would he lower the voting age? "Yes, to six." Then at the back of the crowd there was a disturbance. A heckler was being hauled off by the police. But he had been a curiously muted heckler, a mumbler really; no one had heard him, and the police were carting him off to protect him from Kennedy partisans. The candidate became interested. "Don't take him away," he shouted, "he has as much right to speak as I have." The police started to release the heckler, but the heckler refused. He was a proud heckler and he would not be freed by the word of a Kennedy. "Let him go," said Bobby. But he clung to the police. "Okay," said Kennedy, "if that's the way you want it. But I promise that if I'm elected President of the United States, one of the first things I'm going to do is get you out of jail."

There was, he thought, something comic about him,

a Kennedy, in Nebraska. He would tell audiences, "When I first talked to my advisers about whether I should make this race or not, they said I should. I asked why. They said that if I did, I could come to Nebraska. To run in the Nebraska primary." Later that week at a rally, when a piece of paper fluttered off the lectern and into the crowd, he said, "Give me that back quickly. That's my farm program. I need it." He sensed he was running well, and it was picking up— the results were astonishing. Nebraska, the state they had feared the most, had given him 53 percent of the vote against two opponents. He ran well everywhere, with the Negroes, with blue collar and stunningly well among the angry farmers. (One Kennedy aide believed that the farmers went for Kennedy and not McCarthy because somehow McCarthy was identified with the Democratic party farm establishment, a Midwestern colleague of Humphrey and Orville Freeman. Kennedy, on the other hand, was clearly an anti-establishment figure. This was born out, at about the same time, by a poll taken jointly in South Dakota by three local newspapers. The poll, which seemed astonishing at the time, showed Kennedy beating Johnson and McCarthy, in that order, 52-to-24-to-17 among farmers and ranchers; 51-36-11 among inhabitants of towns up to 2,500 people, and running only 34-34-17 among city inhabitants.

Election night in Omaha, the camp was pleased and relaxed. Pierre Salinger was announcing that McCarthy was dead as a candidate, and Tuck was only mildly annoyed when he heard a network television man announcing ". . . and again it was the classic Kennedy coalition: Negroes, blue collar." "Negroes!" shouted Tuck, "one goddamn percent of the state is Negro." The truth was, and it did not strike them immediately, that they had done well once again in a conservative state. Now on to Oregon.

V

Oregon, the Kennedys would decide in retrospect, was a giant suburb. In disdain, Pat Moynihan, one of their very talented intellectuals (indeed, one of their few intellectuals who actually was an intellectual) would say that Oregon didn't even have crab grass. That was Oregon. Everything that could go wrong for the Kennedys went wrong in Oregon. McCarthy, on the other hand, would be at his best there; his advantages minimized, his assets maximized. The result would be that a Kennedy would be defeated for the first time in an election.

The Kennedys had looked forward to Oregon early in the campaign. It had seemed sweeter and more natural than the seemingly hostile road stops along the way, Indiana and Nebraska. Oregon and California had seemed, in contrast, God's country: liberal, more sophisticated. His staff was sure that Kennedy's liberalism would work well in both places, the staff members after all had been drawn to Kennedy because he was liberal, modern and urbane. They did not, at the beginning, take Gene McCarthy seriously. He was viewed as someone who flowered at a time when he was the only game in town. Now with the real man in the race, McCarthy would wither. But it was not so easy. During the campaign two patterns in white communities had developed: Kennedy was getting the blue-collar people, but McCarthy was running very well among the middle- and upper-class whites. Many of those who were for Kennedy were borderline backlashers who thought the choice in American politics narrowed to George Wallace or Bob Kennedy. They sensed that Kennedy was a tough little Irishman, someone they could understand. One Kennedy aide noted that both Kennedy and McCarthy were Irish Catholics, but they were not the same kind, particularly to Jews. Robert Kennedy was the tough little Irish kid who had punched you in the nose when you were little, while Gene McCarthy was the nice gracious English teacher who said, Yes, Mrs. Goldberg, your son writes very good essays. The Jews felt and sensed this. So did the poor whites; they liked his toughness and combativeness. They felt they could even understand the thing he was doing with the blacks, that was just something politicians had to do. McCarthy had somewhat petulantly remarked, after the first two primaries, that Kennedy could take pleasure in the fact that the least educated members of the society had voted for him.

If the Kennedy trend was true, so was the McCarthy trend. He was running well in the suburbs among both Independents and Republicans. Indeed he and Nelson Rockefeller had a strikingly similar constituency among white Americans. (Rockefeller was much stronger with blacks. He was the governor of a state with a sizeable Negro population, he had run several national races and he possessed a good physical ghetto-style. McCarthy came from a state with a minimal Negro population and he was too fiercely proud a man to make the kind of gestures to Negroes that might have won him their allegiance.) That constituency was middle class and moving up. It was white and it was above blue-collar. Questioned by pollsters about which party it favored, more and more it liked to answer that it didn't vote by party; it reacted to the man. McCarthy appealed to people who were worried about the war, and a little uneasy about the blacks, not exactly against them, but worried about

them. To them he was quietly reassuring: he was intelligent;
he had done the right thing—he had entered the presidential
race and by doing so, he had been above politics whereas
when Kennedy had entered it, he had been playing politics.
To McCarthy's constituency the war was the crucial issue;
otherwise they thought American life was all right. The race
issue was something else. They had been for voting rights
for Negroes, for integration, for the March on Washington,
but they were worried and uneasy now. In the old days they
had turned on their television sets and seen the white Alabama cops—slack-jawed—beating up those nice clean-cut
Negro students, and they had known what they felt, and
that what they felt was right. Now it was more difficult;
the riots, the anger, black people calling them racists—who
me? Someone shot Martin Luther King and that was bad,
but then there was all that rioting and that was worse, and
baffling. McCarthy was reassuring to them; he did not seem
to represent the divisions. But one looked at Robert Kennedy
and he looked a bit discordant—maybe, just maybe, he encouraged them a little, stirred them up.

The quiet man. That was McCarthy. One heard a lot about
the quiet man. The sociologists of American politics, knowing that the new battleground would be in the suburbs, had
taken their questionnaires and tape recorders and had gone
there, in the last few years, to find out who these people
were and what they wanted. At first they had been perplexed.
It was an odd thing for there were no easily identifiable
characteristics for the new candidate. Perhaps they had
been looking for the wrong thing, indeed it might be precisely the *absence* of certain qualities which was reassuring
to these people, particularly because thtey lived in such a
charged up time. That was when the sociologists came up

with the idea of the quiet man. The country, uneasy about
the new passions being stirred up, the growing divisions,
wanted someone to give it quiet confidence. Lyndon Johnson
was not the quiet man, not with that bull horn, nor Hubert
Humphrey, nor Robert Kennedy. But Gene McCarthy, walking down that street alone, throwing away his best lines,
telling everyone how all the experts said his race was impossible because he didn't raise his voice (they didn't raise
their voices either), scoffing at Washington—one sensed
that if elected President he might just abolish the U.S.
Government—was the quiet man. In many ways he sensed
the mood of America better than almost any other candidate. He was an easy candidate to underestimate, and almost everyone had done it; first the President, then the
press, then the pollsters, then the people around him, and
finally the Kennedys. McCarthy's approach was not as
haphazard as it seemed, there was a certain subtle calcula-
tion to it. He ran his own style of campaign very well, and
now here he was in Oregon and Oregon was tailor-made for
him. If he hadn't existed, Oregon would have invented Gene
McCarthy. It liked underdogs up against famous rich candidates, and it distrusted Eastern favorites who wouldn't
debate with poor but honest loners from the Midwest.

Oregon lacked all the Kennedy ingredients. The ghetto,
Tuck complained, consisted of "just one block where the
Reed professors could bring their kids to show them what
one looked like." The Negro population barely existed; the
Catholic population was very small. (There was usually
a Catholic vote for Kennedy though the Kennedy people did
not like to talk about it.) Oregon was beautiful, affluent,
complacent, white, and far from the raw nerve of the rest
of America. It was also far removed from the mood of the

candidate: the challenge that America must be turned around, that the country was in serious trouble. Seeing Oregon one again remembered Barry Goldwater in 1964, remembered talking with him and suddenly realizing that in his hometown the person who drank or committed a crime was just the oddball. He was the offbeat person from an otherwise decent family who, in Goldwater's words, "simply couldn't hack it." There was no connection between crime and restlessness and social injustice. It was simply a very different life. All the great social problems had settled in the great cities of the Northeast and Midwest. There was the migration of frustrated illiterate Negroes from the South, but that problem was thousands of miles from Oregon. "Oh I'm not saying we don't have our troubles like everyone else," one Portland resident told a visiting reporter, "but in ten minutes' time I can be off fishing and forget about them." Oregon generated few of the ugly problems of modern America, and it neither understood nor wanted to understand them. It did not necessarily like what was going on in the rest of America, but it breathed better air and lived a better life. So Robert Kennedy entered Oregon without Negroes and Mexicans and Poles. He had the peace issue but that was a problem too. As the Kennedys would learn again in California, McCarthy had taken away the peace issue and with it the most dedicated, most activist, peace people. The people who desperately wanted Robert Kennedy to make the race six months earlier were now fighting him just as desperately. When peace people became committed they stayed committed. Only two things might have changed them: one was fear of Lyndon Johnson which might have made Kennedy a mandatory candidate, and the other was an even deeper commitment to the ghetto, and that was missing in Oregon.

Now the Kennedys had to deal with this new America

and it was particularly difficult for them because they had always based their races on shaking people up, challenging them, challenging complacency (a Kennedy runs because you need him in these particular times) and in Oregon they felt frustrated. They found the issues elusive; they could not get a handle on Oregon and what bothered its people. Larry O'Brien would recall visiting Oregon in 1960 and sensing the mood and the worries then; but now it was 1968. It was all different; it was all more affluent and subtle. The people who had been blue collar in 1960 were now making $9,000 a year and living in the new suburbs with one and a half cars and two and three-quarters children. "How do you get a handle on a state like this?" he would ask. Indeed about three weeks before the primary, the Kennedy people had a long strategy session with Edith Green, the Oregon congresswoman who was their campaign manager. They discussed exactly these problems; the affluence, the complacency, the undercurrent of resistance to the hard-driving Kennedy style. Someone had turned and asked her: "Edith, how do we do it? How can we shake them up?" She looked up stupefied. "You can't shake them up," she answered.

Everything went better for McCarthy in Oregon. His television money went further and there was more of it. On the heels of defeats in Indiana and Nebraska, there was no inclination to save for California; if he was beaten in Oregon, he was beaten in California as well. So they spent heavily. One minute of prime time in Oregon cost only $350 whereas in Los Angeles it was about $2,000. One radio minute of prime commuting time in Portland was about $18 whereas it would be $65 in Los Angeles. McCarthy had been used to a disorganized staff, but in Oregon he had his best organization: good people had been available early, and he had a good overall structure. As in New Hampshire—unlike Indiana and Nebraska—he again had, because of the war, the benefit of some of the most intense and dedicated activists in the state. The Kennedy campaign was just the opposite. The Kennedys were paying heavily for their late entry. They had been disorganized in general and in order to get off to a running start they had spent far too much time in Indiana, their first domino, and now there was too little time, and they were disorganized. Normally in a national campaign there should be time to organize slowly, to test out people, to try out ideas, to try out speeches without all the full focus of national publicity. Jack Kennedy had had this chance in 1960, and so had Gene McCarthy in 1968, but Robert Kennedy never had that time. In 1968 when he coughed, ten tape recorders picked it up.

Barrett Prettyman, a Washington lawyer, was Kennedy's first campaign coordinator, but that had worked out badly and at a somewhat belated date Bill vanden Heuvel, a wealthy and social young lawyer from New York, was shipped in. This became a point of considerable dispute within the Kennedy camp, for the politicians and some of the eggheads considered vanden Heuvel a social friend of the Kennedys and were dubious about him from the start. This touched on a fairly sensitive area for the Kennedys: Jack Kennedy who had enjoyed clubby people, whose wife disliked politicians and did not want them in her house, had almost completely separated his political and social worlds. Kenny O'Donnell would do the tough political work, but people like Lem Billings or Red Fay would be invited to the White House dinners—people whom Jack Kennedy, as one Kennedy pro put it, "wouldn't have trusted to run a dog-catcher race." There was a certain amount of feeling that this should never happen again. An assistant commented,

"When we came back this year some of us were very determined that this time we would be equals and friends, not employees, and there would be no lords and serfs. We talked about it at the beginning, and now, in retrospect, I think we looked pretty silly because Bob Kennedy just wasn't that way. He wouldn't separate his lives. But the other half of it was that his social friends would come in on politics."

There was always considerable doubt about vanden Heuvel among the pros; perhaps because he considered himself a politician—having managed one campaign for Congress and having had the misfortune to run once himself, against John Lindsay. When things went wrong in Oregon, as they did, the professionals blamed vanden Heuvel. In his defense he claimed that he had been warning the candidate for several weeks that they had very serious problems. But in the eyes of the professionals, Oregon just had not been put together properly: the scheduling wasn't good, the feel just wasn't right. While the Kennedy people thought vanden Heuvel hadn't done enough, some Oregon critics felt that he and his organization had pushed much too hard, made too many phone calls, been too eastern, too pushy. Perhaps if you are going to lose, you are simply going to lose and that's it. Nevertheless the pros were angry about the Oregon organization. "You can walk into an area and tell whether or not it's been organized, whether the advance man was any good, and Oregon was a problem," said one of the aides. "We should have done better than we did. There were too many people at certain levels in the campaign who had titles and slots but weren't really completing their assignments, weren't being pushed very hard."

The lack of organization had hurt them but they had probably been hurt even more seriously by their failure to debate. It was one of the ironies of the Kennedy camp that at the same time they both underestimated McCarthy (in what he was doing, how well he understood the media, and the type of appeal he was making) and overestimated his intellectual gifts. Because of this, they failed to debate in Oregon. It was a costly mistake, for Oregon has its own special style of politics. It is somewhat maverick, somewhat intellectually oriented; and for a variety of reasons it wanted the debate. It believed in debates. The Dewey-Stassen debates had been held there, and the failure to debate was a reminder again and again that it was McCarthy who had entered New Hampshire. The primary is a very big thing in Oregon; it is, said one Kennedy man, "the third largest industry in the state." By failing to debate they were irritating the Oregonians, leaving themselves open to the charges that they had simply muscled people aside with their money and organization, two distinctly non-Oregon attributes. McCarthy played skillfully on the lack of a debate. One of his television clips showed an old photograph of the two men together with the commentary, "This is probably the only time you'll see them together on television."

Within the Kennedy camp, the division over whether or not to debate McCarthy roughly paralleled that over whether or not to enter the race in the first place. The traditionalists argued against it; the young people, again particularly the Robert Kennedy people, argued for it. Walinsky, the most strong minded (Adamant Adam he was called), argued that you had to take high risks; that they had a quality candidate and therefore they should expose the candidate and take the chances. The others had seen what the debates had done to Richard Nixon in 1960. (At the studio in Chicago, Bob Kennedy had looked over at Nixon's picture on the monitor right before the first debate and had been appalled by his color and appearance. Nixon saw him looking and asked if he looked all right or whether he should change anything. "Dick, you look great!" said Kennedy.) They saw a relatively unknown Jack Kennedy destroy the front-running Nixon and they read this lesson from it: the well-known and supposedly front-running Kennedy must not give the unknown McCarthy so much exposure. We have the name this time and they don't; we are in and they are out. Walinsky and the others argued, in turn, that Kennedy had beaten Nixon because he was a higher quality candidate; that, if anything, Kennedy had been too conservative and cautious in the third and fourth debates; that the idea of denying exposure to McCarthy in the year 1968 was an exercise in mythology, the kind of thing the Kennedys normally let their opponents do. Because a fierce two-man race had been going on across the nation for almost two months, the exposure was there, McCarthy was on the news shows every night. McCarthy's very presence in the race had guaranteed his exposure. What they were doing, Walinsky argued, was helping McCarthy maintain his liberal constituency, since the failure to debate fed the idea that McCarthy was intellectually superior and that Bobby was a tough little prosecutor cashing in on the family name and wealth. Finally, Walinsky felt that McCarthy was overrated intellectually; that most of his speeches were of low quality, and most important, because Robert Kennedy bore exposure well, the very same qualities which drew so many bright people to him on a personal level would become apparent to a much larger audience through the debates. If he could impress people like Moynihan, Charles Evers, Harrington, and George McGovern, then he should also be able to impress the average white middle-class voter of Oregon. There was some extremely sound reasoning, but the essence of it was: to gain something you must risk something.

As for the traditionalists, they were somewhat older; they had sampled power. They were with a family which had never lost an election, and the long winning streak had made them conservative, protective of what they had, less willing to risk it. Had they little at stake, and no long winning streak, they might have been more willing to risk it. As it was, they held to the view that McCarthy should try and catch them. (In California Walinsky, who had been highly critical of some of the conservative tone of the campaign in Indiana and Nebraska, felt that Kennedy had been liberated by the defeat in Oregon; that he was a fresher, more relaxed man, more himself. He had been defeated and the aura of never having lost, and therefore of being conservative, was gone. He could now simply go out and campaign and be himself.) There was yet another problem here in the failure to debate, almost a subconscious one. These older men were still Jack Kennedy's people, and they had admired his intellect and Robert's organizational talent. While they realized that Robert had grown, they still didn't entirely believe it themselves; they automatically underrated him just a little. It was still hard not to think of him as the Robert Kennedy of 1960. Perhaps if he went on a debate he would be asked questions which he simply wouldn't be able to answer. Even someone like Dutton— who served as a swing man between the two factions; his ties going back to the older group, his social and political instincts often placing him with the newer one—was opposed to a debate near the end of the primary because he sensed that Kennedy was going to be defeated and he did not want the defeat to come right *after* the debate: That might be a serious mistake, for that would make it a lingering defeat. A myth would grow that McCarthy had beaten Kennedy only after the confrontation, and something like that might cost them California too.

Now the pace was wearing the candidate down. He looked tired and drawn. As if in response to his own fatigue, and the negative reports he was getting, he drove himself harder and harder, a longer schedule, smaller towns. His DC-4 landed on tiny airstrips which could barely accommodate it; at La Grande and Baker, he and his press party were deplaned by fork-lift, at Ontario, by a stepladder. He delighted in using such visits in his openings: "Ever since I was a little boy there were two things I wanted to do: Be a ventriloquist and see La Grande. . . ." The pace was exhausting and one night, as the plane lumbered back to Portland, the reporters began chanting: "Hey hey, R.F.K., how many reporters did you kill today?" Sometimes the very energy of the candidate seemed to offend the Oregonians; it was all too pushy. Even the innocent things backfired. About a week before the primary Kennedy visited a high school in a Portland suburb. About 4,000 students and parents had gathered to hear him, and they were offended by the manner of the press party: reporters shoving their way to telephones, photographers—cameras first—pushing everyone aside to get the best places. They decided that the press's manners were Kennedy manners and the next day, in the school's mock balloting, Humphrey upset Kennedy.

But there were lighter moments. Kennedy had his dog, Freckles, aboard now, and Tuck was in charge of the dog. (McCarthy, hitting harder and harder at Kennedy and his refusal to debate, was critical of the dog and the presence of John Glenn—the apple-pie front—saying, "He's afraid to debate me. He thinks he can beat me with an astronaut and a dog. . . .") Once Freckles got free on an airstrip and Tuck had to retrieve the dog. The reporters laughed and consoled Tuck. It's a terrible thing, Tuck, that a brilliant political in-

tellectual like you is in charge of a *dog*. Don't the Kennedys
have any sense of merit? "It may look like a dog to you," said
Tuck, "but it's an ambassadorship to me." Hearing this,
Kennedy was pleased, and from then on whenever Tuck
made a slip, he'd say, "You just lost Madrid, Tuck."

There were good days too, and the day before the primary,
tired and sensing defeat, Kennedy went into southern
Oregon. This was great outdoors land, hunting territory, and
he had been told by all his advisers that the only issue here
was guns and he was in trouble because of his strong stand
on gun control. (McCarthy was playing this one pretty cool.)
As Kennedy arrived in Roseburg he saw the signs everywhere: "Protect Your Right to Keep and Bear Arms." He
looked around and asked if anyone from the crowd would
like to come up and explain why he opposed gun legislation.
After a few moments hesitation, up came a man named
Bud Schoon, the owner of a floor-covering business and a
director of the Association To Preserve Our Right To Keep
And Bear Arms, Inc.

"Is there anything in this bill which says you can't
have firearms?" Kennedy asked him.

No, Schoon answered. But then he added, "We think
it's a backdoor bill for registration of guns and it will let
the Secretary of the Treasury keep a registry of all firearms
sale."

Then Kennedy took back the microphone, and with
emotion showing in his voice—angered by the fact that
there was so much deception on such a basic thing (there
had been John Birch literature all over Oregon on the gun
bill)—he said, "If we're going to talk about this legislation,
can't we do it honestly, and not say it does something that
it doesn't do? All this legislation does is keep guns from

criminals and the mentally ill and those too young. With all the violence and murder and killings in the United States I think you will agree that we must keep firearms from those who have no business with guns or rifles." But the crowd was not impressed; it was frightened about losing its guns. One man in a cowboy hat booed and shouted, "They'll get them anyway. Someone else yelled "Nazi Germany started with the registration of guns."

"Well I don't think the registration of cars and the registration of drug prescriptions destroyed democracy," the candidate said, "and I don't think the registration of guns will either." He left shaking his head. It was a part of America where the deepest concern was guns, and a fear of what was happening in the rest of the country, a belief that the authorities would take away their guns but permit the rest of America, the bad America, which raped and stole, to keep theirs. Easterners should not be allowed to take away Westerners' guns. Kennedy was depressed by the day and he could sense the defeat coming. The last few days had been a disaster. The Saturday before the primary, the day when you really turn out the crowds so that on Sunday everyone in the state can see and read how you turned it on, had been badly botched. A Saturday morning rally had been scheduled late Friday night, at 11 P.M. It had been organized so late that no crowd could be drummed up, and worse, they had no permit for it so it had to be held outside the city limits. The next stop was next to a carnival and he was drowned out by the noise. His face took on that cold icy look and two other meetings were scratched and he went back to the hotel. He was going to be beaten and he knew it. Humphrey would be the big winner in Oregon. He also knew that this would hurt him in California; the people within the party who opposed him would now have a club to use against him.

The night of the election, as the returns came in, everyone sat around despondently. In the center of the room Edith Green kept watching the early returns and saying over and over again that perhaps it was the lunch-box vote (the non-working class which votes at midday at its leisure) coming in. No one answered her; they all knew they had been beaten. They drafted his concession speech. They were privately bitter about McCarthy's sharp anti-Kennedy attacks and his strange reluctance to attack Humphrey ("He just likes Hubert better than Kennedy," said one McCarthy aide), but decided to avoid rancor; they still might win in California and they still wanted McCarthy's troops. The concession speech was a generous statement; it praised the scenic beauty of Oregon ("one of the most beautiful places in the United States"), congratulated McCarthy on his victory and said that both candidates could take pleasure in the size of the anti-administration vote. Now it was on to California, but he had made a slip there earlier, the kind of slip that more traditional politicians do not make; he had told the Commonwealth Club that unless he won all the primaries he would not be a very viable candidate. Now he would have to campaign in the embers of that statement.

On the plane to California he and Tuck discussed the plan to redistribute the ethnic balance of America so that Oregon could have a ghetto. What can you do about a place like that? Kennedy asked. Airlift in a ghetto, Tuck said. Can you really do it? How many people? asked Kennedy. Tuck did some quick mental arithmetic. Two hundred thousand, he said; with 200,000 the vote will be turned around. He quoted an imaginary headline which gave Kennedy 53 percent of the Oregon vote. "You could airlift in 20,000 a day. But will they *like* it there?" asks Kennedy. "I mean, it's *Oregon,* and all those roses." "We could have a pre-fab ghetto," says Tuck, "have the whole thing brought in. Get to an exterminator and get him to save the rats. Soul food. Give Oregon a little class."

VI ———————————

He flew to Los Angeles from Oregon with the taste of ashes
still in his mouth. Before he could spend too much time
talking about defeat, analyzing it and being analyzed (the
press writing their Kennedy-in-defeat stories: Kennedys
take defeat well), he was back in Los Angeles, into a motorcade, and a tumultuous one. All the people who had disappeared in Oregon surfaced again; the faces were different, the jumpers were back, there were Negroes again. The
motorcade drove through town and as it went, a fat blonde
woman ran alongside shouting, "piss on Oregon, piss on
Oregon." The candidate looked around him and said he felt
like renaming Los Angeles Resurrection City.

California is radically different from other states. It is without traditional organization, rather it is the symbol of the
new rootless, restless America; it tells more about what this
country is going to be in the future than what it has been in
the past. Its suburbs are bigger, and yes, more suburban,
than other people's suburbs; its kooks are kookier than other
states' kooks, and its political extremists more numerous,
more extreme. Berkeley exploded four years before Columbia. California is gaudier, more neurotic, more innovative
than the rest of the country. The ties that bind the older
America, and fashioned its political order, the small neighborhoods, the sense of community; all passed on generation
to generation, are changing slowly in the rest of the coun-

try, but barely exist in California. The people who have broken with all that, the people who were too restless for the quieter America, for whom the small towns never worked, are here, breaking with their families. Californians have broken with their social communities, their ethnic groups (by the time the Poles arrive here, they will no longer be Poles because they don't live among other Poles). It is a strange new society; its politics are media politics; its organizational structure is drowned out by the endless waves of new migration into the state, diluted by the countless new people who move in every month, and who are by and large not poor and not dependent on political organizations for jobs, welfare, and housing. California has a tap dancer-actor for a Senator, another actor for its Governor. California's known, identified political boss, Jesse Unruh, was the first important organization man to urge Robert Kennedy to run and to challenge the sitting President. It is the place where the organization is more fluid and less separated from the political and social turbulence than elsewhere in the country, and where the war was an intense political issue earlier than in most sections of the nation. California has wide-open fluid politics, the least structured in the country. Of California politics it has been said that if you took the 1,000 top Democratic party officials, put them on a barge and sank the barge, all you would lose is 1,000 votes. California is different. It is new politics and Kennedy was glad to be there.

There is a quality of release to California; one senses that at first newcomers either react against it, or join it. The youth of Indiana do not, for instance, live together as freely and as easily as the youth of California, nor do their somewhat older colleagues advertise themselves sexually in the, say, Terre Haute *Free Press* the way they do in the L.A. *Free Press*. The good youth of Indiana might not like

Robert Kennedy but they would be unlikely to view him as a political opiate trying to trick them back into staying in the system (a device of Lyndon Johnson), a system which they feel has failed completely. If they question the system at all, the good youth of Indiana question it very cautiously. The liberals in Indiana, those who worried about the war and were early doves, might have regretted that Kennedy did not enter the race earlier, might have gone with Mc-Carthy. Once Kennedy entered the race, they might have forgiven him, or perhaps being of a strong moral sense, they might have remained loyal to McCarthy. Whichever, they would not, as many of the peace people in California did, turn on Robert Kennedy with all the vengeance of betrayed lovers. He had wronged them; he had failed to enter, then he had entered and challenged their pure hero. With the peace people in California, it was a blood war; it was emotional, for it is probably true of the new media-based politics that the relationship between candidate and constituency is much more emotional and neurotic. This would hurt Kennedy in California; and if it were true about the parents, then it was even more true among the alienated and embittered kids.

Kennedy had sampled some of the intensity and neurosis of California's politics early in the campaign. He had been campaigning in Indiana and had flown out to California for a day and a half—a hectic emotional time. It had started in San Diego when he had arrived; a huge crowd of blacks and whites was at the airport, and among them, a group of young radicals, bitter and hostile. One of them, hearing the rest of the crowd cheer, turned to Pete Hamill, a free-lance writer and a friend of Kennedy's and said, "He's a fink like the rest of them."

Why? asked Hamill.

"He's not talking about revolution. He just wants to

put Band-Aids on the problems. He doesn't want to destroy
the System."

What's the system, Hamill asked.

"Finks like you," the kid said. Paper revolutionaries,
Hamill thought.

At the airport members of the newly formed Peace and
Freedom Party were handing out mimeographed sheets of
paper quoting from *MacBird*. *MacBird*, the play written by
Barbara Garson, accuses Lyndon Johnson of murdering
John Kennedy with the aid of Robert Kennedy. It is considered a fashionable play in radical and even some liberal
circles, though if Mrs. Garson had been a right-winger instead of a left-winger, and had written the exact same
words, it probably would have been considered a less respectable play. The lines from the play went:

> *We must expose this subtle bobcat's claws*
> *He even now collects the straying sheep*
> *And nudges them so gently toward the fold.*
> *O sheep, awake and flee this fenced corral*
> *He's just like all the rest. They're all alike.*

But it would get worse that night, at a rally at the University of San Francisco auditorium. The audience, though
composed of different parts, was dominated by the Peace
and Freedom kids. They were well-organized, angry, bitter,
and they hated someone like Kennedy more than Johnson
or Rusk, because to them Kennedy was more dangerous, he
was the chocolate coating which might lull the others back
to the system. When he entered they were screaming and
chanting, Victory for the Vietcong; Free Huey Newton (a
Black Panther currently in prison charged with killing a
policeman and thus a local radical hero); Victory for the
Vietcong. A kid rushed up and spit in his face, screaming
"Fascist Pig." The face went cold. Kennedy put away his

prepared text, it was the only thing to do, and tried to answer questions. Did you work for Joe Kennedy, someone shouted, getting the name wrong in his excitement, and Kennedy, released from the ugly shouting, laughed. Joe Kennedy, Yes, I worked for Joe Kennedy; he's my father.

Why are you running, someone shouted, and Kennedy traced his involvement in government, the Cuban Missile crisis, the Bay of Pigs. He thought he could make a contribution, he said, trying to save the peace. He wanted to keep America from being involved in other Vietnams.

Victory for the Vietcong, a kid yelled.

Victory for the Vietcong? Kennedy said, somewhat surprised, No, I don't agree with that.

Victory for the Vietcong, the kid repeated. (Later Kennedy told a reporter: those people, the ones who yell Victory for the Vietcong, I can't help people like that, someone who hates this country. Someone who comes up to me, and says, look, this and this and this are wrong, we've got to change it—I can help them. I can understand that, and I can understand some of the bitterness. I can understand the alienation and the eighteen year old black kid who comes to me and says this country means nothing to me, I'm outside it; prove it to me, prove that it's worth it. I can understand that. What has this country offered to a kid like that? Someone like that can be helped. But not the ones who hate it and want to destroy it. How can you help them? It's psychological with so many of them. I can't be their psychiatrist.)

Another kid asked a belligerent question, a question filled with hate spilling over so that in the end one forgot what the question was about and remembered only the hatred and the edge and the bitterness. Kennedy, a little tired, answered, "What we need in this country is to cut down the belligerence. If we let this hatred and emotion control our lives, we're lost."

"It's our lives," one of the kids yelled.

He continued to talk and it got worse; they shouted and booed and yelled for the Vietcong. It was a nightmare evening, he handled it well. Later, when the Kennedy people left, some of the Peace and Freedom kids threw pebbles and apple cores at the motorcade. Bright, upper-middle-class kinds, children of affluence, they believed in the doctrines of the New Left, that if a society is wrong you can do anything you want to redress it, and if someone says something you don't like, you can drown him out and deprive him of his speech. It was an ugly hour, for one sensed that it would get worse, that this was not going to be the last such evening in American life. Later Kennedy would talk with a reporter about it, and talk about the cycle of extremism and violence; that violence and extremism on one side beget extremism on the other. Each somehow makes the other feel that it is permissible and justifiable to do whatever you like.

That night on the plane a group of reporters were talking about the evening, how unpleasant it had been, so much hatred.

"I thought he handled it well," Mankiewicz said.

"But it was so goddamn demeaning," said a reporter.

"So is politics," said another reporter.

A few minutes later someone mentioned the evening to Kennedy. "That was pretty nice back there," the candidate said.

"For a fascist pig you did all right," the reporter answered.

"Yes," he said, "as one fascist pig to another."

Now he was back in California, and all along he had counted on this state to save him. There had been times when it had seemed as if he would be able to take 60 percent in California, though that had been while Johnson was still in the race. Now hopes for sixty were gone, but perhaps in the fifties, the mid-fifties. He had a good base, the Mexicans and the Negroes, but he had to work on the liberals; he was in serious trouble there. Some reports were that he was around 35 percent in middle class liberal districts.

Not among the Mexicans and the Negroes, however. The new complexities, the subtleties of the new politics, were far from their minds. Their issues were survival issues, they were involved in the kind of politics that went back to the early days of the New Deal. Robert Kennedy symbolized to them that America might care. His relationship with the Mexicans was unique; other politicians had courted the Negroes, but no other major political figure had made the cause of the grape pickers his own. That was a special act, for the grape owners are very powerful in the Democratic party. Robert Kennedy, baited a little by his young staff, had finally gone out there, had been moved, and had returned to go to Mass with Cesar Chavez. Could there have been a more symbolic moment? It was the kind of political symbolism which had passed from most of America in our new affluence, the dramatization of a relationship with an ethnic group. Going to a synagogue with Arthur Goldberg would not get back the Jews. It was a momentous occasion; within hours after it had happened, every Mexican American in the area knew of it—it was history. Kennedy had visited the strikers in 1966, had visited the fields and then had held hearings on the strikes. The local sheriff had testified that they were making preventive arrests because they were afraid of violence on the part of the pickets or on the part of the local people who did not like the pickets. The sheriff was very benign about this, pointing out also that he took photographs of all the pickets, and finally Kennedy had looked at him, all the coldness and the controlled anger there, and said: "I just want to ask you one thing. Have you ever read the Constitution of the United States?" The Mexicans had not forgotten. Now in 1968 they would say again and again that he had visited them in *1966;* a great man come to honor their little cause, and now wherever he went, the crowds were enormous. His speeches were terribly simple. Decency is the heart of the matter, he said to them. The death and maiming of young men in the swamps of Asia is indecent. For a man to work with his hands in the valley of California with no hope of sending his son to college, that is also indecent. I think we can do better in America. It was simple enough, but the question had always been whether the Mexicans would vote. Mexicans are bad voters. But they did turn out. In Mexican districts that morning, in house after house, workers came around saying very simply: "Cesar says this is the day to vote for Robert Kennedy." It was the biggest turnout in their history. They voted roughly 15-to-1 over McCarthy, and turned the towns, where anti-Mexican feeling went to McCarthy, into Kennedy camps.

The Negroes would do the same. Kennedy had the Negroes, there was no doubt—it was one of the few remaining love affairs in American politics. In part it was the product of the John Kennedy years. At the beginning of the campaign a poll showed that while only 39 percent of the general population believed that Robert Kennedy "has the same outstanding qualities of his brother," 94 percent of the black people felt that way, an astonishing and quite revealing statistic. It was of course helpful that in an inordinate number of American homes the photographs on the wall were of Jesus Christ, the Pope, Martin Luther King and John Kennedy—but it was also Robert Kennedy himself.

He was drawn to them, felt their cause was the most important thing in America. He did not think one had to go through formal channels to talk with the anointed leaders, but rather he made himself available to a vast variety of black spokesmen. He had listened, was not bored, was not condescending, and they knew this, and were touched by him. He would campaign in the ghettos, always going beyond the allotted time, teasing with the youngsters, asking them what they studied in history, whether they liked school. Who's your favorite president? he would ask. You, you you, they'd shout. No, no, that's not what I mean. He'd grin, he was touched by them. He said to Jimmy Breslin one day in Watts, "These are the best-looking people in the country until they're twelve. You look at the faces. They're alive and have such expressions. What is it? These kids growing up face so many challenges right where they live that it shows in their faces. A character. Then when they get to about twelve, the challenges become too much for them. They get overwhelmed. Then the faces change. They become these masks. But until they're twelve they're marvelous. Much better-looking children than these kids you'd see on Fifth Avenue with their maids walking them."

The affection was there. Every time the candidate entered a ghetto it would begin again, black hands reaching for white hands, a rare enough sight in the America of the late sixties, and he would be very gentle, occasionally admonishing an extra body guard to be more gentle, "Easy Jimmy, your hands are white and theirs are black." But the question always was, Would they reciprocate, would they really go out and vote? There had been a smear campaign at the end. Drew Pearson, who wrote favorably about Humphrey, had written a column saying that Kennedy had authorized the bugging of Martin Luther King's telephone. That King's telephone had been tapped was not exactly news. Everyone in the country, it seemed, knew the FBI had bugged King's phone. The FBI had the tapes and would play them for reporters and for Southern congressmen. It was one of the finer smears in America since there was no way of combatting it; it was the old Communist throttler at his best, saving Democracy for future generations. The column had been picked up by the McCarthy people, and there were radio spots, in a heavy Negro voice, saying, "I used to be for Robert Kennedy, but then I learned about how he bugged my brother Martin Luther King's phone." For a while Kennedy was a little nervous, but then Charles Evers, who was in California speaking for Kennedy, went around Watts sampling barbershop opinion and reported back that it was nothing to worry about. Most Negroes, he said, felt they did not need Drew Pearson to tell them how to vote. One man told Evers, "It's like someone comes to you and tells you your wife is cheating but you love her so much anyway you just don't care."

The mythology of black politics is that Negroes too are bad voters. But there were people in the Kennedy camp who felt that just the reverse was true, that they are very good voters, simply more sophisticated than white people realize. Often they don't care; the choice of two white politicians normally doesn't move them very much and they see marginal differences. Given two candidates whom they measure in degrees of hostility, they will not vote in opposition to the slightly more desirable man. They just will not vote for him either. Thus in Los Angeles they have traditionally voted about 15 percent below the county turnout for whites, with the exception of the 1936 Roosevelt campaign, and the 1950 Helen Gahagan Douglas Senate race (she had been badly smeared on the race question). In 1968 the turnout would prove to be staggering; they would not only vote up to the white level, but in many sections went 5 and 10 percent above it. It is very easy to keep the pressure on in California to get out the vote. There are lists of voters at every polling booth and every hour the list is posted, with

those who have voted scratched out. Thus a poll watcher
with phone numbers can tell exactly who has voted and
who hasn't and can contact those who haven't.

The California people working for Kennedy could not
believe the enthusiasm or number of Negroes working for
him. In 1956 Dutton, working for Pat Brown and needing
precinct workers, had called a number of domestic agencies
and hired workers at ten dollars a head; for this election
there were about 5,000 volunteers. Later, after the vote,
after the assassination, Jesse Unruh would understand what
it all meant. He would turn to a friend and say that that
was the Negro vote for this year. "We can't get them out
again. They'll never come back like that."

But there was a strategy battle over where to make the
effort among the whites. There was so little time, so little
organization. They were already annoyed with Unruh; they
liked him, but they decided his machine was typical of
California, he was a boss without a real organization. "Jesse
was a real poor boy. Came out of the dust bowl. He was very
bright and very ambitious; in fact he reminded us a lot of
a young Lyndon Johnson," one Kennedy staff member said.
"But we had a hell of a time convincing him to broaden the
delegation out. His idea of it was his immediate family, a
few of their friends, his staff people and a few of their
friends. That's not exactly the way to win in California. We
liked him a lot. There's something good there. But sometimes I think we'd have been a lot better off without him,
just going in there by ourselves." Now, late in the campaign,
they were regretting their early confidence and dependence
on him.

In Indiana and Nebraska they had realized they didn't
have the local organization and as such they had no illu-

sions; they had gone in and done the whole thing themselves, made the tough decisions, put their own people in
from top to bottom. But in both Oregon, where they had
what they thought was Edith Green's organization, and now
in California, where they had the Unruh organization, they
had picked up more illusions than anything else. In retrospect, an Edith Green organization just does not exist, or if
it does, it is a highly nontransferable apparatus (except for
the enemies), and they felt afterward that they would have
been better off going in on their own and creating their own
organization. Now in California it was worse, because there
was more illusion and less organization than anywhere
else. Unruh, whom they considered a good man ("one of the
most humane professional politicians in the country," one
Kennedy man called him), had nevertheless been feuding
with the liberals, and they picked up all those animosities.
In addition, he simply did not understand the breadth and
intensity of a Kennedy campaign. "Jesse was always trying
to keep everyone out but his own people, without realizing
it he was really narrowing our base. His theory was a small
operation, and our theory always was that if five people
could do the job, and twenty-five showed up, you found
places for the twenty-five." The California situation, which
had been very good at the start, slipped badly, and by May
the Kennedys had been forced to send Steve Smith and John
Seigenthaler in full time, and had even detached Mankiewicz from the traveling party to work full time in Los
Angeles, his original home.

There remained the growing dispute over where to
make the effort among the whites; among the liberals, who
had turned to McCarthy, in the suburbs or among the white
backlashers. Unruh and his people wanted to go for the
backlashers and the suburbs; it was an area where they
were more at ease and, according to one Kennedy man,

where they "had fewer enemies; so they were pulled that way." But the outsiders, the Kennedy people, wanted to make the effort among the liberals because by all the laws of American politics they felt the liberals should be for Kennedy, and they were uneasy about what would happen if he failed to run well among the liberals in California. It might harden and become part of the permanent political and journalistic ethos of Robert Kennedy: liberals don't like Kennedy and won't vote for him. Perhaps they would never turn it around. The liberal suspicion had haunted him all during this campaign, and it probably was the one thing that got under his skin. It was a product of many things. The liberals, after all, had not changed very much over the last sixteen years, since that first exhilarating Stevenson campaign, and Robert Kennedy had changed a great deal; they found that hard to accept. He had carried on his education in public and his mistakes were a matter of record. He had been the tough lightening rod of his brother's years, handling all the thankless jobs. He liked power, and he looked like he liked power, and many of the liberals, particularly the Stevensonians, drew back from power; there was something inherently evil in power. For the liberal intellectuals, many of them Jews, it was almost an ethnic thing—he looked too Irish-Catholic for them; they believed him more like his father than his brother; and they remained uneasy with him. Their defection hurt him the most. He had gone through it all once before, wearing a yarmulke all over New York City, sensing the strength of their distrust, but finally winning their votes if not their affection. Now in the campaign the Jews were retaining all the old suspicions, and this hurt him. Again and again with friends (at times, half of his advisers seemed to be Jewish) he would ask why it was happening and they would try to explain. But I thought we had established a relationship,

and then they did not come across, he said. Some of the
McCarthy support he could understand, he said, but now
some of these people in New York and California, people
who had asked him to make the race, were for Humphrey.
Humphrey. Someone said not to worry, that if he got the
nomination they would all come home. It's not the same
thing, he said; if they vote for me against Richard Nixon,
what does that mean? What kind of consolation prize is
that?

Now in California, his advisers suggested that the
major effort be to court the liberals. The Kennedy people
thought the Unruh people looked down on the liberals and,
more important, underestimated them as a force in California politics. There was a group of people which the
Kennedys grouped as intellectual-liberals-academic-profes-
sional-people. They were roughly one half Jewish, said a
Kennedy aide, and the rest might just as well be; they had
the same voter profile. They equaled about 8 percent of the
California population, 4 percent Jewish, 4 percent non-
Jewish, but since they were almost all Democrats, they
equaled about 10 percent of the total Democratic party. But
since they voted with a special fervor, they represented
roughly 15 percent of the voting Democrats, and since they
were respected and influential, they could carry satellites
with them, making a total of 20 percent. But in early May
they were for McCarthy in roughly a 2-to-1 ratio and so a
major effort was initiated to swing it around the other way.
A collection of very distinguished liberals was imported to
talk to small groups, coffee klatches, synagogues—always
looking for groups which were either anti-Kennedy or fence-
sitting. In they came, Pat Moynihan, Robert Coles, Arthur
Schlesinger, Michael Harrington, Edwin Reischauer, Roger
Hilsman, Roswell Gilpatric, Cesar Chavez (for white liberals). On one campus, Moynihan was speaking about the

Negroes, and up came the question, What about wire tapping. Moynihan, too busy with the blacks all those years, didn't really know about the wire tapping. But he happened to look up and there was a sign which said "Alexander Bickel will speak here at 2 P.M." and he said, well when Bob Kennedy was appointed Attorney General, Alex Bickel had called it the worst appointment in the history of the republic, but when Kennedy left office he wrote in the *New Republic* that Kennedy had the best record on civil liberties of anyone in years, and now he's speaking here today for Kennedy and if you have any questions you can ask him.

In a sense the strategy probably worked. Some of the Kennedy people thought it was a waste of manpower, and that the guests didn't reach enough people, but the general feeling was that they had made ripples beyond expectation for Kennedy. McCarthy still carried the liberal areas, but by a much narrower margin. The problem, of course, was California's rootlessness. The California experts remained dubious about the idea of the imported speakers. Yes, sure, they spoke to a group of fifty people, and those fifty people had fifty wives, and fifty friends to whom they could say, "Well, you know, I had a pretty interesting talk with that Pat Moynihan, and he told me some things about Kennedy I didn't know and I want to think about this election a little longer." But finally, even those many converts, if they were all converted, would be too few. The Unruh regulars, of course, wanted a more traditional campaign, and had more confidence in the efficiency of their organization than the outsiders; but they were all bewildered by the same question: how do you reach the people?

The people had come to California and lost their roots, their dependence on one another, their knowledge of and ties with their neighbors. They no longer lived in the neat little neighborhoods in which they had grown up. California was a long way from Thornton Wilder's *Our Town,* another country. (One wondered what Wilder would do with the new America of California; would he sound more like Harold Pinter?) Now their new relationships came from the media—it existed, it was dependable, it was there every night, and had certain known, identified, friendly characteristics. They knew and felt at ease with the talk shows— Merv, Johnny, Joey—and inevitably California politics became media politics; it was the only way of reaching into those great disorganized scattered neighborhoods. So Kennedy now turned, for guidance on how to run a media campaign in California, to Dutton, the expert on California politics who had helped run those surprisingly successful early Pat Brown races. Dutton, not a close friend at the start, had grown closer and closer to Kennedy as the campaign developed. He had always been one of the brightest men that the Kennedys had brought to Washington in 1961, bright, talented, honest but modest. He lacked a capacity for self-glorification and dramatization and he was not nearly as widely known as he should have been. Dutton fashioned a television campaign which everyone in the Kennedy camp agreed was the most brilliant ever done in California—until afterward, when they realized what McCarthy had done, and realized that he, a rank outsider, had done it better.

There are three major television markets in California: the San Francisco area, the Los Angeles area, and the San Diego area. Traditionally a candidate would arrive in California, spend a day in Los Angeles, then the next day on to San Francisco, and then the next day on to San Diego. But Dutton had changed that; jet travel was so simple these days that they would begin in San Diego in the morning, fly to another market in the afternoon, and finish in the third market area in the evening. That way they would touch all three major markets in one day, and the local television stations would all rush out and get the scene: candidate arriving, jet coming to a halt, candidate shaking hands, jostling of the airport crowd, into town, five words from his speech; it was free television time in all three areas each day. They were all pleased with this. The candidate told people often Fred Dutton had the best political judgment of anyone he knew, and they were very pleased until they realized what McCarthy had done.

McCarthy could not draw crowds the way Kennedy could. Where Kennedy would draw 15,000, he would draw 1,500, and he knew this, and the press knew this, and nothing would irritate him more than to read the stories the next day where the press would judge him for his crowd gap. The crowds bored him anyway; he did not like the grabbing and the thrashing; and so rather than be judged badly on something he didn't like in the first place, wearing himself down, burning up his time and energy, he skipped crowd stops as much as he could and went instead on the radio shows and the televisions talk shows. There are hundreds, perhaps thousands, of them in California, and there is a great secret to getting on them—show up at the studio. The proprietors, of course, are delighted, and by and large it is the sweetest kind of questioning in the world. Good morning Senator, could you please tell us what a hell of a good guy you are and what your fine record is. Then, fifteen minutes later, Thank you Senator for taking the time to come by and explain to us what a terrific guy you are. And this was McCarthy at his best, witty, sometimes gentle, being a little nasty about Robert Kennedy. Suddenly the Kennedy camp realized what had happened. There would be two minutes on television each night of Robert Kennedy being mauled, losing his shoes, and then there would be fifteen *free*—that was painful—minutes of Gene McCarthy talking leisurely and seriously about the issues. That Gene McCarthy, the people would say, is a serious man; and the quiet man had turned a liability into an asset. Kennedy could draw crowds, it was one of his special strengths, and he was tied to doing the crowd thing. McCarthy was not able to do the things of the past, such as draw crowds, and thus was freer to take advantage of the new things. Now the Kennedy people realized that McCarthy had run, perhaps not by intention, a better television campaign in California.

In a somewhat modified form, this had bothered the Kennedys earlier in the campaign. The TV men covering him would always shoot him with the crowds, good stuff though rarely of substance, and the film clips would come in to the great networks. On that particular day McCarthy would do little because there was little in the way of crowds, but in order to have *something*, he and the TV reporters covering him might do small-spot interviews so that networks, who would not want to run Kennedy without McCarthy, would have something to balance the Kennedy coverage. So again they would portray a mauled Kennedy and a serious thoughtful McCarthy. A few days later the Kennedy people would want to show a Serious Kennedy and, in the morning, they would summon a TV man and give him a small exclusive, serious interview; then they would all go out campaigning and the crowds would maul Kennedy and the TV men would shoot that too. Both cans of films would come in to the networks and since one can was action, it was also *news*, and it would be used and the interview would be thrown away. In desperation one of Kennedy's aides finally told him that if he wanted to be serious and thoughtful he would have to stay in his hotel room all day and be serious and thoughtful there.

But now the campaign was almost over, and he was driving himself relentlessly. Just these few more days and he could ease off, reduce the twenty hour day to a sixteen hour day, a fifteen stop day to a four stop one. He rested only for the great debate with McCarthy; the debate was to be on a Saturday night and on Friday he told an aide: "I'll have my biggest crowd of the year out here tomorrow."

"No, no," said the aide, "you have the day off except for the debate. We canceled everything off."

"No, it's my largest crowd of the year," he insisted. "All my advisers are flying in from all over the country to tell me what to say. It'll be a hell of a crowd." He was in a good mood.

The debate, like most highly promoted things in American political life, such as conventions, contained less than met the eye. It was not a debate, it was a love-in; they had no great dispute. They complemented each other: McCarthy would fire Dean Rusk; Kennedy would not deal in personalities. McCarthy wanted only the exposure that went with challenging Kennedy face to face; Kennedy wanted only to soften the ruthless image which had built up against him. It was a mutually pedestrian performance, and as far as convincing people went, it probably had a marginal effect; most people would watch it and see what they wanted to see and hear what they wanted to hear. *The New York Times* editorial page gave it to McCarthy; I gave it to Kennedy. It seemed to me that the great issue of the campaign, at this point in California, was not Vietnam or ghettos, but Bobby himself. He succeeded in softening the issues against himself; he did not look ruthless and he seemed McCarthy's intellectual equal that night though even the announcer seemed both men's intellectual equal that night. But now it was over and there was precious little time left. McCarthy was blitzing now, coming on hard with a strong television campaign. There are only two ways of doing your television programming: either you save up your television money and blitz at the end, or you spread it out evenly. McCarthy, who was less well known, decided to blitz hard at the end, pound away with the name right before the election. It was the right strategy for him, the Kennedy people acknowledged, whereas with Kennedy the problem was different; he was already well known, so they spread it out more evenly to ease the ruthless issue.

The mood in the Kennedy camp was becoming a little more optimistic and more relaxed. Abba Schwartz, who had handled immigration in the state department, came out and helped work with the Chinese and had explained to some of the Kennedy people how to vote the Chinese. Tuck had answered, yes, that was fine, but the only problem was that two hours after you voted them you had to vote them again.

They were convinced now that they would come out of the state running hard, so all through the California campaign they hammered away at Humphrey, the enemy. It was good politics; implicitly it said that McCarthy was not a serious figure, and this was helping to ease some of the Eastern liberal feeling against Kennedy. For McCarthy was slightly trapped; he had to run against Kennedy to stay in and he was doing this, sharply and caustically, but the impression was growing among some of McCarthy's foremost supporters that he was too hard on Kennedy and too soft on Humphrey. Clean Gene, among some of the kids and some of the intellectuals, was becoming tarnished for the first time.

For some reason Oregon no longer seemed so final; Kennedy's advisers sensed they were going to come out of California with a real chance. They had already evolved a fairly sophisticated post-California strategy; a national

grass-roots television campaign would be mounted, which
would be similar in some ways to the one Rockefeller finally
used, except much less emphasis would be on newspaper
advertising and more on television. They would have five-
minute spots five nights a week, right before the 11 o'clock
news: *This is Robert Kennedy and I want to talk to the
people of the nation just as I did to the people in the states
with primaries*. Then finally one long thirty-minute program, virtually a speech by the candidate, spliced in with
documentary shots of the public life of Robert Kennedy.
Then an intense travel schedule from California to New
York where the New York primary was to be held June 18,
and where the Kennedy people were in serious trouble
fighting a well-organized peace campaign. (As in California,
the best people had gone over to McCarthy, and they had
the best slates; he was still fighting the late entry.) Then
from New York all over the country, a schedule arranged
by Sorensen; twenty-six states where the delegates were
still flexible. They would stop by in Chicago. "A good meeting with Daley. We'll be very respectful, very polite. Here,
Mister Mayor, is what we can do, where we run strong,
and here's Humphrey's strength and McCarthy's strength.
All very polite. Then we'll go into the ghetto and get one
hell of a response." Then a quick flying trip overseas to show
that a major American political figure can still be acclaimed:
Robert Kennedy Wildly Cheered in Paris, Rome, Warsaw.
All of this, of course, designed for crowds, for publicity, for
impact, and mostly to touch the polls and thus the delegates.

They felt that the delegates could still be wooed. Humphrey
was far ahead in delegate strength, but Kennedy did not
believe that it was a particularly strong hold; indeed Kennedy and the people around him sensed that Humphrey's

position would go not up but down as the convention approached, and this, his strength, would erode. They believed that much of Humphrey's resurrection was tied directly to the euphoria of the Paris peace talks and Johnson's magnanimous gesture. That had taken place on March 31; it would last for six or seven weeks, but then, as June moved along and July arrived, the euphoria would end, the old malaise about the war and about the administration would return. By early July it would be the new Hubert and the old war and the old malaise, for Humphrey was tied directly to things which were outside his control and which looked insoluble. (Although the Kennedy people felt the Humphrey delegate counts were inflated, they deliberately refused to challenge the figures. There were two reasons. The first was that they thought Humphrey's grip was soft and they did not want to alert the Vice-President's people to this until after the primaries when it would be too late. The second reason was that they were sure that after the primaries there would be erosion from Humphrey's total, and they were anxious to create a reverse bandwagon psychology for the Vice-President.) In addition, Kennedy thought McCarthy's hold on his young people was bound to slip. There were already signs that it was slipping; the Oregon campaign, with its attacks upon Kennedy rather than Humphrey had given rise to some disillusionment.

So he pushed harder and harder. The Monday before the California primary he put in the final, most bone-crushing day of all. He covered 1,200 miles of the state, touched every ethnic group, and made a triumphant visit to Watts. Teasing with them, he said, Yes, you come out to see me. Are you just going to wave to Mr. Kennedy and then tomorrow when I'm gone forget about me, or are you going to vote? I think you'll probably forget about me. The exhaustion showed; in San Diego where he spoke to a rally—

divided into two sections because there were so many people; 2,500 in the first seating, 2,500 in the second—he col-
lapsed momentarily between speeches. But it was a strong
day. The response of the crowds encouraged him, and at
one point while discussing why he was running, he said,
"My first responsibility is to the United States, not to the
Democratic party. It is a responsibility to the country itself.
Now, feeling as strongly as I do, I can do nothing other than
what I am doing."

Election day. A good day. Enormous Negro and Mexican
turnouts. The results were very good; the day was looking
better and better. Early in the evening the results came in
from South Dakota, and they were impressive; indeed they
may have spelled the beginning of the end for Humphrey.
South Dakota, where Kennedy had spent so little time, is
Humphrey's backyard—a rural state and the vice-president's birthplace—and now it was giving Kennedy 50 percent, McCarthy 20 percent, and a Johnson slate, which was
pledged to Humphrey, only 30 percent. It was astounding
news, a staggering victory, and Kennedy knew this would
have a powerful effect on Daley. Humphrey could not even
run well in his own region, where he is best known. It was
one of the least-noticed political events of the year, but a
persuasive piece of evidence, and Kennedy immediately and
joyously recognized its significance. Earlier in the evening
he had talked with Dun Gifford, a young lawyer on Teddy's
staff who was helping to handle delegate counts. He had
asked him about the delegate counts and Gifford said they'd
be assembled for him tomorrow, "and you're going to like
them." Curiously, they had gotten better since Oregon; the
defeat there had taken the edge off some of the hostility
toward the candidate. It was a remarkable thing, Oregon

had made him more attractive. "Don't try and kid me with delegate counts," Kennedy said. "I used to do them myself." Now the air was expectant and the early results were good; they showed Kennedy winning a major victory. One of the networks said it would be 54 percent, a smashing victory. Not sixty, but with South Dakota it was enough to remove most of the stigma of Oregon. His spirits were buoyant. Earlier in the evening Pat Paulsen, the new television comic, had referred to Humphrey as Herbert Humphrey ("I will debate all of the candidates for President in a place of their choosing. I will even debate Herbert Humphrey in a smoke-filled room"), and that caught Kennedy's fancy. It somehow seemed to fit Humphrey and now, grinning, he said, "I'm going to chase Herbert's ass all over the country. Everywhere he goes I'll go too." Then he descended to acknowledge his victory, to talk about the violence and the divisiveness, and to let a nation discover in his death what it had never understood or believed about him during his life.

ABOUT THE AUTHOR

Born in New York City thirty-four years ago, DAVID HALBERSTAM graduated from Harvard in 1955. For five years he worked for newspapers in Mississippi and Tennessee before joining *The New York Times* in 1960. As a foreign correspondent for that paper, he served in the Congo, Vietnam and Poland, and his dispatches from Southeast Asia won him the Pulitzer Prize in 1964.

Mr. Halberstam is the author of *The Making of a Quagmire*, an account of our commitment in Vietnam, and of two novels, *The Noblest Roman* and *One Very Hot Day*. For the last eighteen months he has been a contributing editor of *Harper's Magazine*, covering the American political scene.